Mindspeak

Tapping into Sasquatch and Science

Christopher Noël

Perhaps the most significant discovery within quantum mechanics is "entanglement," a phenomenon that Einstein called "spooky action at a distance." These connections are instantaneous, nonlocal, operating outside the usual flow of time and space. They imply that at very deep levels, the separations that we see between ordinary, isolated objects are illusions created by our limited perceptions. Reality is woven from threads that aren't located precisely in space or time. Tug on a dangling loose end from this fabric, and the whole cloth twitches.

— Dean Radin, *Entangled Minds: Extrasensory Experiences in a Quantum Reality*

The people who've never experienced it, they just look at you like you're a crazy person. But the people who have experienced it, they look at you and smile and say, "Yeah, we know."

— Wayne in Michigan

Also by the Author

*Next of Kin Next Door: How to Find Sasquatch a
    Stone's Throw Away*

*A Field Guide to Sasquatch Structures:
    The 50 Most Common Types in North American Forests*

The Sasquatch Savant Theory

*Electric Sasquatch: How a Natural Force May Explain
    "Supernatural" Powers*

The Girl Who Spoke with Giants (novel)

*The Mind of Sasquatch and the Secret to Their Success
    (A Theory)*

*Our Life with Bigfoot: Knowing Our Next of Kin
    at Habituation Sites*

*Sasquatch Rising 2013: How DNA Breakthroughs and
    Backyard Visits Reveal the Greatest Story of our Time*

In the Unlikely Event of a Water Landing (memoir)

Doctor White's Monkey (stories)

Table of Contents

Preface
Part 1: My Experiences in East Texas

Through the Looking-Glass......................9
Test 1..12
Test 2..13
Test 3..13
Test 4..14
Test 5..15
Test 6..18
Test 7..18
Chatting with Nantaya........................20

Part 2: Mindspeak Testimonials

Overview...25
1. Rich Germeau: Washington State..........27
2. Denise: Maine................................33
3. Connie: Iowa.................................41
    4. Connie's Daughter Tracy..............44
5. Sophie: Nova Scotia.......................49
6. Wayne and Todd: Alaska, Michigan......57
7. Connie Willis: Oklahoma..................67
8. Les Stroud: Tennessee.....................71
9. Stewart: Oklahoma.........................75
10. Ann: Minnesota.............................87
11. John: California.............................93
12. Paul: West Virginia, Pennsylvania..........97
13. Thom Powell: Oregon......................109

14. Elizabeth: Texas.............................111
15. LeeAnn: Ontario…......................121
16. SnowWhiteBigfoot: Ohio..................135
17. Robin: Michigan, South Carolina,
         Texas….................................139

Part 3: Experimental Evidence

Beyond Magical Thinking......................167
Senders and Receivers...........................171
The Sense of Being Stared At..................173
Reach out and Touch Someone...............177
Entangled Minds...................................179
Uri Geller...183
Remote Viewing....................................189
Adventures in the Hive Mind.................195

Part 4: How are Such Things Even Possible?

Matter and Consciousness......................205
What are Nonlocality
         and Entanglement?......................211
Is Mindspeak Fishy?..............................215
The Right Receiver................................219
The Intelligence of Things......................225

Part 5: Links to Autism

Exposure Anxiety..................................231
Very Special People...............................235
"It Just Comes to Me"….........................241
A Brain Upgrade….................................245
Fields of Knowing…...............................249

Creatures in the Field...............................251
A Dance of Distraction..................................259
Fruits of the Gift 1......................................263
Fruits of the Gift 2......................................267
Big Bang, Back Yard....................................273

References..275

Preface

Telepathy sometimes occurs between members of our species. For some reason, our next of kin, the Sasquatch species, seems to possess this capacity to a much higher degree.

I'll stick my neck out first.

In Part 1, I will share what I experienced in East Texas several years ago. It will sound like a fairytale; I can assure you it *felt* even more so to me.

My expectation, however, is that as you progress through this book, the startling events described in Part 1 will seem more and more plausible within the broadening context of others' testimonials (Part 2), solid experimental evidence for telepathy (Part 3), and a discussion of the scientific framework within which this phenomenon may begin to make sense (Part 4).

Finally, in Part 5, I will link the telepathic gift to those gifts associated with autistic savants; that is, I will show how a higher incidence of psychic ability among these rare individuals relates back to our forest-dwelling neighbors, given their own apparently species-wide form of autism as outlined in *The Sasquatch Savant Theory*.

When first experiencing mindspeak, many assume they must be going crazy; as you'll see, Survivorman Les Stroud worried he was manifesting symptoms of schizophrenia, and Wayne in Michigan even asked himself, *Am I having an aneurysm right now?* I hope this book will serve to ease such anxieties and reassure people that they are quite sane and healthy — even lucky.

If you yourself have experienced mindspeak, you can join the cause and help to spread the word about this remarkable aspect of reality. Write me at MindspeakBook@gmail.com, and if your account meshes with the contents of this book, I will include it — with your permission — in an updated version.

Christopher Noël
Northeast Kingdom, Vermont
March 11, 2019

Part 1
My Experiences in East Texas

Through the Looking-Glass

Alice laughed. "There's no use trying," she said, "one can't believe impossible things."

"I daresay you haven't had much practice," said the Queen. "When I was your age, I always did it for half an hour a day. Why, sometimes I've believed as many as six impossible things before breakfast."

— Lewis Caroll
Through the Looking-Glass

I always try to keep an open mind, but this was a tough one. What could be more far-fetched than telepathy? Here's what: telepathic communication with *Sasquatch*?

But when you work with people at habituation sites — places the large species tends to visit — you get very accustomed to references to "mindspeak." Typically, at least one family member will report regularly experiencing this phenomenon, seeing images spontaneously arise in the mind's eye and/or hearing a voice in the head. Moreover, the mindspeak often develops into a *two*-sided conversation, the in-house residents able to ask questions and receive replies.

For a long time, I'd reflexively set such claims aside, mildly annoyed to have to deal with *this* kind of thing from otherwise rational human beings. I was eager instead to learn about the concrete, real-world, flesh-and-blood facts of the habituations — when the visitors show up and when they don't, how they behave, how they treat those who live in the house, types of communication that occur, etc. But the same testimonials kept coming up with stubborn consistency, and in locations hundreds or thousands of miles apart, spoken by witnesses who had never compared notes with one another.

It wasn't until I actually visited and spent extended time with one of these habituators claiming telepathy—a woman in her fifties whom I call "No-Bite" for reasons given in my book *Our Life with Bigfoot* — that I was able to take the direct measure of this wild proposition for myself. It certainly helped that she was anything but wild; instead, she was the soul of sincerity, always taking care to explain herself clearly and patiently and never once trying to *sell* me on what she was experiencing. She'd had Sasquatch activity at her house since the middle 1990s, while raising her daughters, but her mindspeak had only begun in 2007, a year before we met.

From 2008 to 2011, during five visits to No-Bite's little house in East Texas, we'd hear them tree knocking and whooping, mostly at night, in the surrounding forest. In

Site of the footage, the next morning. In the foreground are the ashes of the bonfire; in the background, not far away, the woodpile.

November, 2009, I even managed to capture one on video with my thermal camera as she spied on us from behind a woodpile less than thirty-five feet away.

See YouTube: "Woodpile Sasquatch."

According to No-Bite, this was the very same individual that she'd been communicating with mentally for about a year.

"How did it start?" I asked.

"I'd been experiencing Sasquatch visits for years, and then one day a friend, who is psychically gifted, told me that there was one particular individual here named Nantaya. He suggested I just call her by name in my mind and see what happened. So one day I decided to give it a try. I thought: 'Nantaya?' And immediately I heard, *'What!?'* It was a clear female voice in my head, and she sounded annoyed."

This jarred No-Bite's worldview just as much as you'd expect.

I'll admit I was captivated. I pitched myself into the sheer speculative *fun* of it; I mean, nothing ventured, nothing gained, right? Yet of course I didn't have the foggiest notion how such a thing as this could be actually, *literally* true.

Over time, I ran several tests…or they were run *for* me by circumstances. My friend didn't mind; she gladly participated because she was free of doubt.

Test 1

I asked her whether Nantaya might have any advice for me on where to investigate in my own research area, back in Vermont. No-Bite looked into space and then returned with, "Directly east of you: big water."

"Yes, twelve miles east, that's where a young man saw the seven-foot, hair-covered man running through the woods."

I had never mentioned the direction or the presence of that body of water. I'd interviewed the witness and visited the exact spot of his sighting.

"And she says you should not look on the side with the dirt bridge, but the other side."

Yup, that's exactly where the sighting occurred. And that's where I later recorded six hours of wood knocks on May 18, 2009. And no, I had never shared with No-Bite that this body of water is a reservoir, with a dam constructed of earth — a dirt bridge.

Test 2

We'd be sitting on her front lawn at night, and she would be silently "talking" with Nantaya in her head. Pointing, No-Bite would tell me, "Okay, her group is coming up from over there now, south of us." And sure enough, a few seconds later, dogs in the same direction would start barking frantically. This happened quite often.

Test 3

This one I planned long in advance. Back in Vermont, I'd snapped a picture of my front lawn with lush birch and maple trees at the height of summer, then I'd had it blown up and laminated and brought it with me here to brown, drought-stricken East Texas. I wanted to share my home world. I made sure not to show it to No-Bite before she and I took an evening walk down a dirt road. I had the picture inside my shirt, flat against my chest.

Out of the blue, Nantaya asked No-Bite to ask me to please hold the picture up for her to see; how did she even know I had a picture? She says she is across the field to our left. It was about a hundred yards to the dark tree line. I positioned No-Bite behind me; as far as she knew, it could be any image in the world. I then held the image up in front of me, raising it toward the distant forest.

Immediately, behind me, I heard my friend's voice, speaking for Nantaya: "So *green*! Is that where you *live*?"

Well, my good old trusty skepticism was now rapidly deteriorating.

Test 4

Indoors, No-Bite and I watched an NBA Finals game, Miami vs. Dallas. June, 2011. During time-outs, I trotted to my car, parked near the chicken coop and goat house, to make preparations—changing the batteries in my audio recorder; making sure the memory card had enough room; mounting the thermal camera snugly in the back, passenger-side window—but I did this in brief bursts of activity rather than one long session, because I didn't want to arouse suspicion from the woods.

On one such foray, I climbed in the driver's seat and switched on the dome light in one motion. After a minute of double-checking the audio recorder, I killed the dome light. What the *heck*? In the backseat, my flashlight was burning bright. I hadn't used it since the previous night, and even if I'd forgotten to turn it off then, the batteries would have been well dead by now, more than twenty-four hours later.

In the house again, I asked No-Bite, "So…do you know if they've been to my car?"

She looked off into space. "The young one was in the backseat."

I got a little chill. "Did he…*touch* anything?"

"No buttons!" she blurted, then laughed. She reported that one of the juveniles had once had a bad experience touching buttons in a car, and so this had been forbidden ever since.

"Right," I said, laughing along, "it wasn't exactly a

button." The on/off switch on the flashlight was the kind that slides. I told No-Bite what happened.

After quizzing the young one, Nantaya said that when the light came on, he got scared and ran.

"How old is he?" I asked.

"Seven years."

Test 5

Over morning coffee, I asked No-Bite whether the young one might have paid me a visit last night, where I slept in my rental car.

"He bounced your car from the back," she said. Only later did I find the evidence of this.

Directed where to look, No-Bite crossed her backyard and found something placed on an overturned white barrel, not far from my car. She picked it up and handed it to me. "This is from the young one. He wanted to put it in the car, but the Big Man said, 'That's enough with the car!'"

It's a piece of petrified wood.

"She says he found it in a fast-running river."

On the way to the airport, after thanking my friend, as always, for her hospitality, I stopped for gas, and that's when I noticed them—a set of fingerprints on the hatchback, where someone had "bounced the car."

Luckily, the car was black, so these strange remnants really stood out, representing digits clearly smaller than my own...and much pointier.

These prints seemed deposited by fingers uniformly covered in dirt, or dirt mixed with oil. An alternate explanation was that my own fingers could have left "latent prints," which then picked up blown dust or pollen. Yet, besides the size difference, another objection was that during my week's rental of this car, I'd opened and shut the hatchback many times, certainly leaving lots of prints, but this morning's discovery showed just one set from a right hand, and another, two feet away, apparently from the left hand.

The clearest finger on the right hand (below) showed side striations that don't appear in human print patterns —

Striations marked

check it for yourself; and see YouTube: "Sasquatch Fingerprints: East Texas Habituation Site."

Test 6

On the way to her house, May 30, 2011, I'd bought cakes at Walmart, a cheesecake and a red velvet cake. After cutting half for us and half for Nantaya, and then grouping the halves onto a plastic-hooded plate, No-Bite and I walked it up the dirt road and left it on the flat-topped fence-post.

When I returned the next morning, the post and surroundings were empty of plate, plastic hood, and cake. Back at the house, No-Bite reported that she could distinctly feel Nantaya holding her head and moaning, "Owww... owww...oww...I am *poisoned*."

"What?!" I said. "We'd never poison you."

"Oh," No-Bite realized, "it must be the *sugar*. A sugar headache." She could feel a dull, throbbing echo of it herself.

"What part of the cake did you eat," I asked, "or all of it at once?"

"No. First, I ate the red one, and that was good, it didn't hurt me. Later, I ate the other one. It was like mud in my mouth, but without stones." The cheesecake. "Owww... owww...*owwwwww*."

Test 7

On the morning of June 5, we sat on No-Bite's front lawn, finishing our last coffee together before I had to leave for the airport in Dallas.

It had been a brutal six days, topping a hundred

degrees each afternoon.

I asked, "Can you ask Nantaya if she could make some kind of goodbye sound for me? It would make me so happy."

No-Bite: "She says to wait."

During my visit, we'd probably spent twenty-five hours sitting here at this exact spot, under the shade of her hickory tree, and not heard a single knock, even faintly, from these surrounding woods. Such have come only at night.

I was thinking, *"She says to wait,"* eh? *Yeah, sure.*

But within ten seconds…SMACK! from a hundred feet away through dense forest, over my left shoulder. So close.

I found I couldn't breathe correctly. No-Bite and I gaped at each other. I slapped my hand on my chest and called out several times, "Oh my God!" and *"Thank you,* Nantaya. I will hold that in my heart forever."

No-Bite said, "She's laughing!"

That single solid rap of wood on wood had swatted away my last shred of resistance, like a grand slam home run, and the implications were vast and unavoidable: Mindspeak is quite real; Sasquatch can use it to exchange thoughts with certain humans; Nantaya is not a figment of my friend's imagination but an actual creature living in the woods with her own kind; and I filmed her that night behind the wood pile.

Chatting with Nantaya

The most sustained conversation I had with Nantaya (through No-Bite) occurred the day before that, June 4.

Chris: How should we handle our curiosity about your race as it grows?

Nantaya: There is aggressive curiosity and gentle curiosity. Get to know us like you get to know a new neighbor. You don't go in a neighbor's yard, cut down the neighbor's trees. You don't take the neighbor's children. Peaceful curiosity is not a problem, just don't try to take us over. Your children have a gentle curiosity, that's why we come to them; they're not a threat. We've been interacting with children in the hopes that eventually we CAN come out.

Chris: Why would you want to come out?

Nantaya: So we don't have to be in fear. This has been going on since the days of the wagons. Your people were afraid the natives would steal their children, but part of the time it was US interacting with them. Children would step into the woods and sometimes they'd come back, sometimes not. The children would go off with us and PLAY with us. We've been hoping that if we teach your young ones, they will still know us when they grow up.

Chris: Do ALL of you share this goal of being able to come out?

Nantaya: Some yes, some no. It's like having a

Dangerous secret: Sometimes it's good to come out, sometimes it's bad. The more the hairless ones know about us, the more dangerous. Even when the secret is out, there will still be places the hairless ones can't go.

Chris: But wouldn't more understanding make the secret less dangerous, too?

Nantaya: More knowledge means more danger, because not all people use the knowledge the same way. If I told you we all like peanut butter, some of you would use peanut butter for bait, some for friendship. But that's not the secret.

Chris: The motivation of No-Bite and myself and many others is to shed light and increase the peace.

Nantaya: Yes. We won't ever be able to come out everywhere, because it's not safe. Why the Big Man is so worried about my interaction with No-Bite is that we never know who's going to come here. At what you call "habituation sites," you are always being tested — what you do with gifts, who you tell, what chain reaction occurs. Habituation clusters are happening all over the place, but it is a more recent thing. The native peoples knew we were here and respected territories. But as the settlers came in, they didn't respect boundaries, they just took over. When there was respect, there was less need to test hairless ones all the time. Now we have this new problem to deal with. The settlers and now their descendants keep invading — they see a place they like, they build on it and destroy it. You clear the land because you are fragile. Weak. You can only fight with weapons, not rocks or sticks or bare hands.

Chris: More and more of us today are finding out about your race, but much of what's being said is untrue. If you could speak to the human race, what would you tell us?

Nantaya: The best thing I can say is "DON'T." Don't harm the little ones. If you see one little one, there are definitely more. Don't assume anything. Don't think because you know one of us that we are all the same. Don't think because you know many of us that you know the personality of all of us. Don't seek us out because we will hide. Don't avoid us because if we want to find you, we will. Don't think we are stupid because we will embarrass you. Don't think we are intelligent because we will make you appear foolish. Don't feed us because you think we are starving, because we are experts at hunting — you feed us, it's because you want to share. Don't hunt us because you cannot catch us. DON'T.

Part 2
Mindspeak Testimonials

Overview

The following testimonials represent a wide range of mindspeak experiences, from subtle to overwhelming. You'll read about a woman informed of her son's car accident minutes before the police show up at her house; about another who is powerfully led to a hidden riverbank where she finds pristine Sasquatch tracks; about a man who, after clashing with an angry male, is told in no uncertain terms never to pursue them again; about a boy who hangs out with a young female for years without quite realizing that she's not of our species; about a young girl who is drawn from the safety of her room, across the backyard, across a muddy field, and is then met by a hairy family that gives her the choice to join them or to return to her mother; about a man who attends a Native American drum-making retreat, only to undergo a life-changing encounter in the nearby forest; and about Survivorman Les Stroud, suddenly struck "right in the middle of my head, right *inside* my brain, the strongest-ever voice that was not my own. It just said, 'If you want to meet us, stay the night.'"

Individual relationships to mindspeak differ markedly, both from person to person and within the arc of a single life history. Elizabeth reports a gradual evolution from emotional impressions to vivid mental images to fleeting thoughts (apparently not her own) to distinct voices in her head; Robin's communication constantly fluctuates among all these types; Sophie, Connie, and Stewart heard voices from day one; while Rich Germeau, Ann, and LeeAnn never receive images or voices, simply a sense of "deep knowing."

The moral tenor of these communications can run from compassionate and loving to dark and ferocious; both Paul and Robin narrate this stark dichotomy.

Their time frames vary as well. Sophie, Robin, Connie, and Connie's children have been interacting with Sasquatch for decades, since childhood; Paul had intense encounters as a young boy but nothing since; Rich Germeau, Les Stroud, Denise, Stewart, Connie Willis, and brothers Wayne and Todd did not experience any psychic connection until well into adulthood.

Of the seventeen testimonials included here in Part 2, eleven are the result of interviews I've conducted with those involved. The other six come from sources cited in each case. There are an eighteenth and nineteenth testimonial (also transcriptions of answers to my questions) included in Part 5, where they fit with the topic of autism.

1. Rich Germeau: Washington State

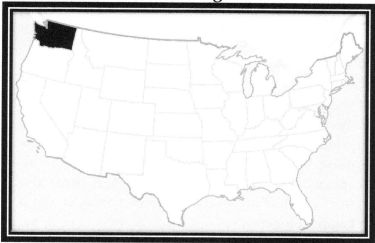

This testimonial appears in the video "Bigfoot: Rich Germeau discusses an encounter on Harstine Island" on Greg Brotherton's YouTube channel. Notice the shift from a purely and powerfully emotional experience to a more mental one—a clear message received at precise intervals. Versions of this same transition from heart to head occur repeatedly here in Part 2.

You know, most Bigfoot researchers, they tend to ignore all this woo-woo stuff. They only take in "legitimate" stuff within their acceptable belief system, and they tend to throw everything else out the back door. But unfortunately, about sixty percent of the evidence is all that stuff they want to throw away.

So I started hearing about these things and I just wasn't into accepting it. I mean, I'd take it into account because I was talking to people that I really trusted over a period of time, and they were stuck on these stories of this weird stuff. I just kind of chalked it up to…they're eccentric people. Let's face it, people who are having ongoing encounters are not normal people; they're a little different, but I took it into consideration because otherwise I figured I wasn't doing myself any justice as an investigator.

As time went on and I kept putting cameras in places and trying to hide them and trap these things to where there's no way they could know it's there, and there's no way they could avoid getting caught…but they *do*, every time. I became more and more accepting of [their abilities] and having less and less faith in the technology and tactics I was using, because I knew I was doing everything right. (I'd captured lots of pictures of mountain lions and wolverines.) I knew I was where I needed to be, except it wasn't coming together.

Finally, how it all peaked out was when I'd been working at this location on Harstine Island. We started it in 2008, following a report at this location where these renters were at, along the road, North Island. It's in an area where we were able to look back through the BFRO database, and in a decade, there were eight or ten sightings of them crossing the road in this same spot. Harstine Island Drive North. And more than once, there were multiples seen, and by all different people, either going home or just driving through the island, but always at night.

One day, November 11, 2010, I went to check the cameras. I had five game cameras in this one area, a really small area, in this alleyway between residential neighborhoods. It stretched for about a mile and a half down to a beach. I didn't have my gun with me, which was rare. I almost always carried it. Not for Bigfoot, just because you never know, and I was a cop so I carried a gun at work anyway. I do think there's significance to the fact that I didn't that day.

From the minute that I pulled in there, I had this strange feeling. That I shouldn't be there. That I should just go home. But there was no reason for me to pay attention to that intuition, so I ignored it. But as I checked the first camera, got the SD card and re-armed it, I kept feeling unsettled. A feeling of *dread*, I'll call it. It's like the whole world was starting to get really close around me. Like there's no time anymore, everything has stopped, and the world is pressing down on you. It was overcast and slightly drizzling, but quiet at the same time. No birds, nothing.

So I walked from that camera and went down to the second one about seventy-five yards from the road by an old outhouse. So I'm checking this camera and my awareness really gets heightened, and I'm just sensing all kinds of weird stuff and *not feeling right*, feeling like the world is going to end, but that's so out of context. There's no reason for it. Just feel bad. Not sick or anything. It's nothing I've ever felt before or since then. It kept building and building and building.

I have like twenty-five keys on this ring, and I'm going through these keys [to find the right one for the chain around the camera], and every key I'm checking, I feel more of a sense of urgency to leave. I kept hearing twigs break off to my northwest. This area is covered by cedar trees, and the limbs come down real low so you can't see in there at all, but I keep hearing something snapping twigs, and it sounds close, but I keep looking and there's nothing there. Nothing.

Why am I so afraid? I'm seventy-five yards from the road. There's cars driving by. There are no leaves on the trees. Nobody is going to come grab me and drag me away. There's no danger, but I feel that there is. But logically there shouldn't be.

I keep going through the keys, and I'm feeling more and more afraid. What is it? What is going on here? There's something over there. I keep looking for something to satisfy me, like it's a known thing. I keep hoping something comes out. And then I hear this loud HUFF!, which I've heard before. Oh, it's just a deer snorting, right? I'm a little relieved. It's from the same direction as the snaps. It's rut season, so I'm thinking it's a buck and maybe I'm going to see it in a second, but I don't.

I get to the second-to-last key, and it opens the chain lock. I've got my head down, working with the camera, and I hear a loud groaning exhale, *very* close. The groan was like disappointment, disgust — that was the tone of it. Like it's just frustrated…making you aware. And it was right in front of me now, which caught me off guard because it had moved, or it was another one. I'd never heard anything from this new direction at all. Later, I figured that the one snapping twigs was diverting my attention, while the other one was super-close to me the whole time.

In my mind, I kind of already know what I'm about to see, and as I'm lifting the brim of my hat up, I can see there's something standing up alongside of a big alder tree about twenty yards away, and his head was about as high as those ferns.

As I'm lifting up my head, it knows I'm going to see it, so it already starts to kind of duck down to about a third of its height, and in the same motion it shoots across this opening but facing me the whole time. It was huge. I could see there was stuff stuck in its hair, twigs, and it was really big and bushy. And it was frightening in its speed. And it was silent when it moved.

When it got out of sight, dead silence, so I'm assuming it just got out of my view and stopped, because I don't see how you could make it through any of this thick stuff without making a lot of noise. There's just dead and broken trees everywhere.

Pretty much immediately after that happened, something started happening to me every night for two months straight. I'd wake up at 3 AM, every morning like clockwork. BAM, I'd sit up wide awake, and I'd have a very strong impression: *Stop looking for them. Stop doing cameras.* Never any consequence included, just *stop.* It was always 3 AM on the dot.

One night, toward the end of these two months, I stepped out of my car and a Sasquatch screamed at me — high-pitched scream twenty feet from my car right across the street from my house. And I live in a residential area. There's a lot of greenbelts and stuff. This was clear as day, volume ten, meant to let me know, *We know where you live.*

I'll tell you that since then, I've gone out in the woods a little bit but frankly, I feel extreme guilt when I do, like I'm not supposed to be doing it. And no consequence has ever been expressed, at least no feeling of any, because I've tried to seek that out, to find out why. I just feel really strongly that I'm not supposed to look anymore. I have a real intense feeling, and I have it right now when I'm talking to you. That's all I know about it. I don't think I'll ever do research again in the sense of going out to seek them. I'd never think of using technology, cameras or anything, again. I think that that would be insulting. The quickest way to piss them off.

I can tell you the whole thing's weird. The stories are weird, and they happen over and over again. And it happened to me.

2. Denise: Maine

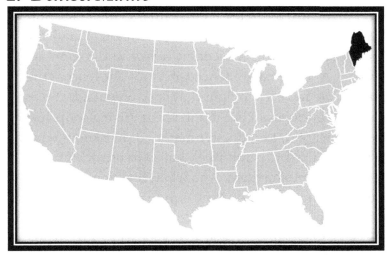

Here, the experience escalates gradually from a typical backyard encounter, through an emotional (fear) phase, like Rich Germeau above, and finally into the reception of a clear voice in the mind.

I honestly didn't believe they existed because I'm a naturalist. I like animals and nature, and I like science. So when everyone was talking about it, I thought it was just a species they hadn't discovered yet, and maybe they saw something that is not what they thought they saw. Some type of an animal.

So that was my thought until one day in 2015. I started loading up my shed with yard sale stuff from my house. I was going to have this big yard sale. At about 2:30 in the afternoon, this rock hit the shed, and it hit hard. You gotta understand, in the back of our house is hundreds of acres. There are no houses. And we don't have them on either side of us, and we're way up off the road. So I came out. I was alone, and I thought, *Oh my god, there's some weirdo in the woods*. So I yelled out to the woods, "I've got a gun!" And I ran toward the house. "I'm gonna get my husband!"

And then…it started happening at night. I had big dogs I would let out, a Siberian husky and a German shepherd. And we have a fenced-in yard. The fence is five feet high. We have a spotlight that I put on outside. So as I'm letting my dogs out one night, I hear this big snap. Just because I'm a girl, that doesn't mean I didn't know what size it was. I used to climb trees. I used to break branches when I was climbing them. And it was like eight feet high, because of the height of the sound; it was that close. Branches would snap *loudly*.

I'd go, "Okay guys, c'mon, everybody in." I'd call my dogs in. So this kept happening every night. And then it got more and more and more. It would snap eight feet high. Dead silence. Go eight feet over. Snap. But every time it walked, you couldn't hear it. It was like it just snap…distance…snap…distance. So I'd go, *Okay, that's bizarre*. And so I'd go in the house.

Well, at one point I asked my son, "Please come out with me." It's like 9:30 at night. I said, "I just feel like there's something weird out there." My son was fifteen at the time. He stood out there with me, and I'm not kidding, whatever it was in the woods just went crazy. It made this big knock, like it took a metal bat and hit a tree. It was so loud. And I'm like, "Oh my god! Let's go in, let's go in. I don't know what that is out there." Me and my son went in the house, but we lost our hearing for like fifteen minutes, that's how loud it was. Me and my son are trying to talk, trying to yell at each other in the mudroom, going,

"What was that?" And we're trying to hear each other. We were just shaking, it really shook us up.

This went on steadily for four months, every night, and it got to the point where I started to write a journal. I wrote the time, the date, and the weather. Because I just couldn't wrap my mind around what kind of animal this was. I ruled out moose. I ruled out bear. I ruled out deer. By the fourth month, I stopped asking my son to come out with me, because every time I did, it got worse out in the woods. We heard stick clacking. We heard hitting the tree real hard. And we heard this thumping that sounded like it was underground. It was the freakiest sound.

So I had him go back in the house, and I said, "You know something, it's every time you come out. I don't think you need to come out anymore. I don't know what's going on, but it doesn't like you out there with me."

There was one big night in 2015. I'd usually go and do the flashlight scan to see if there were any porcupines outside the fence. My husky booked it out there because it smelled something, so it pushed me, and I went, "Crap! There's something out there." So I ran out there, barefoot, it's summertime, in August, and I see a porcupine running for the woods. Then I see the other porcupine running up the side of the tree. So the shepherd went for the one going up the tree, and the husky wanted the one going into the woods. And I yell for my son, "Get the shepherd in!" and so he got the shepherd in, and he stood outside waiting for me as I went barefoot with two flashlights, because at the far corner of the fence it's darker, the spotlight doesn't hit it as well. My husky was so focused on that porcupine, he wouldn't look at me, he wouldn't listen, and I'm going closer and closer to the dark and I'm like, "I don't want to go over there." And I'm talking to my husky as sweet as I can to make him come to me, and I have a tiny flashlight in each hand, and I go, "Honey, please come to me...*please.*"

And all of a sudden, twenty feet into the woods, it's dark, but you can see someone in the trees, and I hear this THOOM! Like a giant foot hit the ground. And then, it went vibrating up my legs. And I went, "Uhhh, oh my god!" And I've never seen my husky ever tuck his tail between his legs. He was just flying by me like a white blur. And I'm still standing there, and all of a sudden I feel something coming at me, and it was massive, and I thought I was going to die. *I thought I was going to die.* And I went, *Oh my god.* And I just stood and froze and it hit me. My arms flew up beside me and I screamed. It was like a vibration hit me, and I tried to turn to run, and my son screams at the same time, and he says, "Did you see that? Did you see that?" And I'm still running across the yard, and I said, "What did you see?" And he goes, "Something like a brown light went right by your stomach, Mom." He saw like a football-shaped orb. And I went, "What?" I was so confused. I said, "Get in the house! Get in the house! It was a bird, just get in the house." Because I saw his face was so scared.

And so I got in there, and I stood in the mudroom, and my whole body had...like...*electricity* in it, and I couldn't stop shaking. And I started crying, and my son started crying. He goes, "What's going on with you?" I go, "I don't know! I can't stop shaking, I can't stop shaking. "

You're going to think this is crazy, but I think they build up energy in them from the earth, like electric, then it bursts out into an energy, but we see it as orbs.* Well, it didn't stop there.

My son and I went in the house, and it was about 11 o'clock, and he said, "Mom, I'm okay now. I can go to bed now." I said, "Okay," so I picked up his dishes he left in the living room, and I started to go by the stove to go to the sink and out of the vent I hear this deep moaning, like he was so sad, and he had the lung capacity beyond anything I've ever heard. I said, "He can't breathe that long." That is not a human. That is not a coyote. It was crazy. I just never heard something moan so long.

But it wasn't just that. All of a sudden, I had a vision of what he was doing. He was sitting with his knees up and his head down, and it was like he was showing me he was sorry. And then I stood back and I put the dishes in the sink and I went, "Oh my god, what just happened? What am I seeing? What is going on?"

I stayed up for another couple hours. I kept bouncing around *What is out there? Should I protect my family?* I didn't have any answers. So then I started feeling better and I thought, *Well I'll go to bed now*, and it was about 2 o'clock then, and I put my head on the pillow. And then I heard a voice.

---

* Witnesses report seeing these "orbs" quite commonly in association with Sasquatch activity; more about this phenomenon later. On the Rocky Mountain Sasquatch Organization YouTube channel, see "Orbs Captured at Seven-Time Bigfoot Sighting Hot Spot"; on the Brown Dwarf channel, see "Orbs and Super Moon," "Strange Balls of Light in the Woods," and "Is this Orb Reading my Mind?"; and on the Mattsquatch Presents channel, see "My Orb Story."

I open my eyes and I go, "Oh my god, what was that?" And it was like deep, but it was a female, and I go, "Okay," and I close my eyes. And she goes, "Here," and I open my eyes again, and I go, "Oh my god." And she did it to me four times, and then she said, "I am letting you know you're not sleeping, so you know you can hear me now."

It went like this. She showed me that he was her teenager. He went too far. He wasn't supposed to. He stepped over his boundaries. He got too close. She was saying that he was hanging around me. And this is the thing: She will talk but she will also show pictures. Also, she will make you feel what she's feeling. She will make you feel like you are in those moments, inside what's going on.

So I'm getting all this, I'm getting overwhelmed, and it's like she's very attuned to me, and when she realizes she is doing that, she makes me feel calm so she can continue. She sensed that I was getting too much energy from her. I have not told my husband this. He believes in my abilities, but to be able to *talk* to something out there? I know he couldn't wrap his brain around that.

It was like she could tell what I was going to say before I said it. My emotions, and empathy, and sad, and curious, when I was about to ask her a question, she would already answer it. That blew me away.

This is where it got scary for me. She showed me her two-year-old, who was like four feet high. But she only showed her silhouette sitting beside him. She was sitting on a log with her head turned to the right. Her partner (the male) was to the left of her. Her teenager was behind her. So she's showing me this. She said, "He does not know I am talking to you. He will do what he must do."

And then I was feeling *his* energy through *her*. Then she realized I was feeling it too, so she pulled it away. It was pictures where the protector sees men coming in with guns, and he will protect his family and do what he must do. And then she shut off the vision. But I was still feeling it, and then she pulled that away from me because I started shaking, and she didn't want me to see what he would do.

She repeated that over and over, and that's what got me more scared: "He will do what he must do. He will do what he must do. He will do what he must do." And I thought, *Oh my god, what?* I think that's why to this day when I have to let the dogs out at night, that little scene is still stuck into me. *He will do what he must do.*

And then, it was like an overwhelming love she gave me. Then she took me...like we could fly over the earth, and through countryside. It was gorgeous, it was beautiful. And then she said, "More will see us. More will hear us. It is time." She did this with words, plus she did it visually. It's like she could make it so we could become one. I've never had this happen to me in my life. "People with good heart will hear us. It is time. The earth is hurting. We need to communicate. We need to protect the earth."

Later that night, there were high-pitched whistles, and I lay there in bed and counted them. There were three long, three short, three long, three short, and she did it eighteen times. The long ones were *so freakin'* long, it just blew me away.

"We will be coming through when the last leaf falls." She repeated that three times too. To make sure I heard it.

A structure Denise found in the forest behind her house.

3. Connie: Iowa

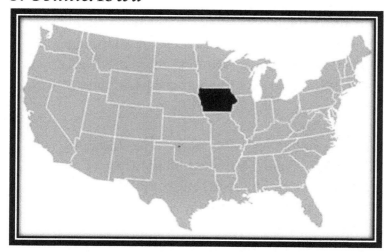

This account demonstrates another common pattern — sporadic communication over the years with long periods of silence. I was fortunate to be able to interview three family members (below) who have experienced the same Sasquatch group. You can read more of their habituation experience in Our Life with Bigfoot *with Bigfoot, pages 47-59.*

I was seven years old and taking my four-year-old brother to the outhouse. He ran on ahead and then came back saying there was a bear in the outhouse. When we got there, there was no bear inside, so while my brother was using the toilet I was swinging on the door and that's when I saw it, standing behind the outhouse.

I remember thinking, *That's a really big one, whatever it is*. It was male and just stood there looking at me. In my head, I heard "Don't be afraid." That was the first time with the mindspeak.

Around the same time, I was berry-picking with my grandmother. We always had to be at the spot by sunup. That's when we saw three of them standing at a distance, picking and eating blackberries. There were also what we called dewberries — like blackberries but a lot bigger. So there were three of them standing there picking berries when Grandma and I got there, and she told me not to be scared of them.

I said, "Why?"

And she said, "Well, they're just like Indians." (My grandmother was part Shawnee Indian.) They didn't seem to be afraid of us, and evidently she could mindspeak with them at that time. She told me they would put pictures in my mind and not to be afraid when they did. I didn't ask anything. I just took it for granted that she knew what she was talking about. My grandmother…she'd expect you to remember what she said and not ask questions.

Later, when I was a wife and mother, we lived in a great big brick house, and one of my sons had his headphones on, listening to music, and he suddenly said, "What did you say?" It was a warm fall day so we had the windows open. He said, "What do you want, Mom?" He was in the southeast corner of the house upstairs. He said, "Who hollered my name?"

I said, "I didn't call you."

Then I heard *my* name hollered, and I asked my husband, who was downstairs, "What do you want, Dennis?"

He said, "I didn't say anything, but I heard someone yelling your name."

It was verbal, out loud. When I talked to the neighbor lady, who lived about a quarter mile down the road, she said, "Wasn't that really strange last night?"

And I said, "What's that?"

And she said, "Oh, Bud and I were sitting outside, and the corn was rustling, and someone kept saying my name and it was like it just floated over the top of the corn."

After that, three times, I heard my name being called in my *head*. Nobody else heard it. Just three times, that's all.

A few years later, we moved about two miles down the road, and that's when I started hearing my name called again. I'd be out on my deck and I'd say, "Yes?", but that was it. At first I kept thinking that I was just hearing things. I would also get grunts and other sounds.

This house was really close to the river. We lived in the river bottom, and at first I assumed it was somebody yelling, and it was echoing back and forth or something. And then, out of the clear blue sky one day, I was sitting at my sewing table, and all of a sudden I could not see what I was sewing. I saw this picture of a big female Sasquatch with a baby and two others with babies standing not far from her. It was just like they were *there in front of me*. I stopped the sewing machine.

In this vision, they were in the timber. I call the woods *timber* because that's what we call it here. They were standing in the timber and they weren't far from the house. I knew the particular area where they were at. That's when the female started talking with me. Told me not to be afraid, to come out, that they were just like us and lived in a clan or group. She would tell me things, and it was like talking with my grandmother. I never questioned my grandmother, okay? I didn't talk to this Sasquatch. I mostly just listened. She would come and talk to me. Her name was Shepinga. She talked to me—just simple things, very repetitive—for several years.

She told me she was my neighbor, and I thought, *Wow*. When I saw her with my mind's eye, she looked mostly gray, a blue gray. But then when I finally saw her in real life, she was a brownish beige.

4. Connie's Daughter Tracy

At first, I wasn't sure they really existed. Mom and my siblings had seen them several times before I did. It wasn't till my late thirties that they started putting pictures in my head, but different than what others got. The first time was when [researcher] Abe del Rio had come to visit, and we were sitting on Mom's back deck. I got this really weird feeling like there were multiple of them around us. It was pitch dark, and I told Abe, "Hey, you've got to get on this side of me. I don't want to be here on the edge."

He's like, "Why?"

I said, "It's really weird but I'm having these pictures. But it's from their direction. They're looking at us. And there's more than one because it's coming from different angles." It was like in a movie where you jump from one viewpoint to another. I could look through the trees. I could look down at the ground. And I was seeing us sitting on the deck. I put my hand up and felt like this cold vibration. It freaked me out.

Later, back inside the house, we were all talking, and I said, "That was the weirdest thing I've ever had happen. I don't understand how this can be in my head but looking at us sitting on the deck. I think I'm losing my mind."

Abe said, "I don't think you are, Trace. There's a lot of people that experience that."

About six weeks after this, I went to Mom's for coffee. We talked and I told I'd been having more weird stuff happen. Like I'd hear a bird chirping at the window and when I'd look over there, it would stop and no bird, then when I went to put on my shoe, it would start up again. Over and over. Also, I'd been having these thoughts that didn't seem like my typical thoughts. I was trying to deny them. You don't want to have thoughts you can't control, you know? I said, "I think I'm losing it."

Mom said, "I don't think you are. I think you're just letting your guard down and they're trying to communicate with you."

So I'm getting ready to leave for work from her place. It was probably eight, eight twenty. I back out of her driveway and start heading down the road, and all of a sudden something catches my peripheral vision. I think it's just the corn, the wind maybe blowing the corn. Nope. It's a red Squatch. He was standing off by a tree, behind the barn, but he was out far enough in the open that you could see his hair blowing in the wind. He was maybe two trailer-lengths away, like sixty feet. Mom had always told me, "It's when you least expect it that you're going to see one."

So I stopped and just kind of watched him, and we made eye contact. I wasn't scared. He just stepped back into the trees, and I didn't see him again.

But after that, I wasn't so scared of those extra thoughts in my head. I felt like I could crack open that door. I'm a little more open to listening to what comes into my mind, and I actually talk back now. It's gone from pictures to a voice, or not quite a voice, more like mix of thought and voice, going, *I'm here*. Other stuff, too, but it's hard to say what is *said* because it blends in. But still, it's different enough to know that it's not your own thoughts. Like I wouldn't think, *We're over here by the river*.

Back to Connie

When my granddaughter Jessie was about fourteen, they started calling her from the timber. "Jessie! Jessie!" and it scared her. I told her not to worry, they wouldn't hurt her. Then, they started calling her a Native American name meaning "mourning dove" and putting pictures in her head, and she could also talk with them mentally like me.

When they would mindspeak with me, I never experienced headaches, but my son Tony did.

Her little brother Spencer, when he was five years old, would always go down to what we called the junk ditch, a big washed-out spot that we'd fill up and then every few years bulldoze it over. There ended up being a little cave down there. When I'd go for my walks in the morning, I had three horses and some dogs that would follow me. When we'd get down there, the horses would take off and most of the dogs.

We had a hundred and twenty acres, and Spencer was a free spirit. I'd say, "Now you stay up here away from that junk ditch or the Junk Ditch Monster will eat your butt." It was just like he was drawn down there all the time when he was young. One day, he said he was going to go outside and I was kind of watching him, then I had a phone call and got preoccupied, and he was gone. Soon, I look out the window and here he comes, and he's coming from the direction of the junk ditch, and I said, "Didn't I tell you to stay away from that junk ditch? The Junk Ditch Monster will eat your butt!"

He just laughed and said, "No he won't, I already talked to him. We're friends." That threw me. I didn't know what to say to that.

But they didn't start mindspeaking with him again that I'm aware of till he was a senior in high school. He was staying with me and working at Subway, and he wouldn't get home till midnight. He knew that the young ones liked him because every time he'd walk up to the house from his car, they'd throw stones and walnuts about two feet in front of him.

One night, he came in and was sitting down and eating a sandwich from work. Then, he laid the sandwich down and said, "Oh, Grandma."

I said, "What's the matter?"

"Someone is talking to me in my head and they're using *my voice!*"

I said, "That's a Sasquatch."

He was telling Spencer to tell me he was sorry for breaking the "water stump." See, we had a tree farm about five miles from us, and we had a water hydrant that had gotten broken, and my husband blamed the kids for breaking it. He ended up having to dig the whole thing up and put a new pipe in and everything. The Sasquatch told Spencer that they traveled through there quite frequently.

When Jessie was eighteen and about to go off to college, I had cancer in my ear and had to have my mastoid removed. After that, I couldn't mindspeak with them as well anymore. They just put pictures in my head every now and then. One afternoon, a few days after I got home from having surgery, I thought I was hearing something but I wasn't sure. It was garbled. All of a sudden, here comes Jessie around the corner and says, "Grandma, you've got a bunch of Sasquatch out here wanting to talk to you. You better go see what they want!"*

---

* Jessie is a high-functioning autistic person. See her testimonial in Part 5: Fruits of the Gift 1.

5. Sophie: Nova Scotia

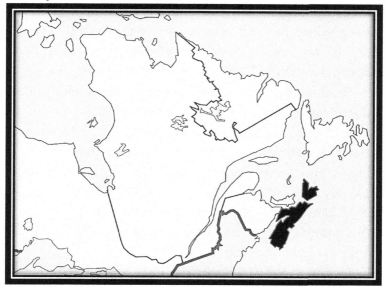

This girl found herself in a situation that boggled her young mind but one that is not, after all, very rare. Many children in Sasquatch proximity are contacted by our forest cousins, and, free of the mental clutter of later years, they often prove exceptionally permeable to mindspeak.

I was four or five years old. We lived in a row of cottages that was next to a farm in the countryside. Behind the house was a hill covered by a forest, and there was a dirt track that led up to the top of this hill. I would often leave toys on the back porch that would go missing and then end up on the roof of the coal bunker, which was like a small shed out back next to the garden. I would blame it on this boy that lived a few doors down, and he would always swear it wasn't him. There were also things that would go missing and then end up in the garden later on. My mum would be weeding the flowers and say, "Oh, here it is. You must have left it here" when I knew for a fact I'd never played with it there in my life.

At nighttime, I would hear noises up on the hill in the woods. In my mind's eye, I was seeing a party of teenagers. It sounded like a real ruckus going on up there—loud shouting and what sounded like males and females, distant voices you couldn't make out.

I would go to my bedroom window, look up at the top of the hill expecting to see firelight or torches [flashlights] moving around, but nothing, no lights in the woods whatsoever, yet all this noise. I could also hear what sounded like trees being pushed over. My mum could hear the sounds too, so they weren't just in my head. She blamed it on kids from the town.

This went on for two or three nights, and I remember every night going to the window. One of these nights, I was lying in bed, and I felt drawn to go look again even though there were no noises at that point. I felt almost magnetically drawn to go back to the window. That's when it felt like there was a voice in the back of my head that was calling to me, and it felt kind of strange. It felt like it was pulling me or allowing me into a meditative state of mind. I remember it felt like I lost about ten minutes, but when I looked at the clock a whole hour had passed.

The next morning is when it all happened. I was in my bedroom, upstairs in our cottage, and I could see the edge of this forest and the hill. This was late morning. I remember playing in my bedroom, just playing with toys, and there was like a voice in my head that was telling me to go to the window, and I remember thinking it was strange but feeling compelled to do what it said anyway, so I went to the window and my eyes were drawn to look up to the forest on top of the hill. As soon as I made eye contact with the forest, I felt like something really gripped my mind, and it was a female voice in English that told me that I should walk up the hill to the forest.

Then, it quickly started flashing images. It painted the picture in my head like a movie of the future of me walking out of the house, going up the dirt track, through the field, and towards the woodland. And then…it showed me seeing *them*…and then, it flashed me back to sitting in my bedroom, looking up there, at the beginning again.

So while they're showing me the actions I should take in sequence, there was a voice in the background telling me, "It's okay. You're not going to be harmed. You'll be safe. We're friendly." That's why I felt like I should do it. Also, I thought, *I need to see if that really does happen if I follow those instructions.* So I put my shoes on and went outside and walked up the dirt track. My mother probably didn't know how far I went and probably just assumed I was in the back garden.

I remember going out and going up the dirt track and stopping maybe halfway up, then having a flashback of the vision I'd had in my room and being impressed that there were rocks on the ground that matched up perfectly with the image in my mind. I had walked up that dirt track in the past, so it's not like I didn't have a memory of it, but it was just *exact*.

When I got to the top of the hill, the same thing happened again, and then when I came to our gateway into the field, which was all plowed and muddy, I hesitated to enter, because I remembered from the vision that what happens next is I see *them*. Right in the moment, I looked maybe five meters ahead at a puddle, and in the middle was a toy of mine. It was a puppet, not a fluffy puppet but made of rubber. I think they were called Boglins. They looked like goblins and they were just silly puppets with googly eyes.

It was just lying in the puddle and I couldn't fathom how it got there. I walked over and picked it up, and before I knew it I'd been tricked into walking into the field. At the exact moment that I would have maybe decided to not go. It was like it was placed there to lure me that extra step, like they'd already predicted this would all come true.

So now I'm standing at the middle of the field and there's a hedge at the far end, and behind the hedge is the forest. And in the middle of this hedge, there's this gate that's opened up with a dirt track that leads up into the forest.

Just left of this gateway, behind the hedge, stood a family of four Bigfoot. I didn't know the word at the time,

I didn't know Sasquatch. I'd never seen the Patterson/Gimlin footage on TV or anything. So I didn't know what these things were. They just looked like hairy humans, kind of like gorillas in a way. I remember the one that really caught my eye was this adult female, and she was looking at me with these warm, motherly eyes. She had a very black face and short black hair, and she was very thick (just like the Patterson figure I saw years later).

Clinging onto her left arm was a young female — maybe eleven if you compared her to a human--who was obviously the daughter of this mother, and she was clinging very shyly and hiding her face in her mother's arm, only just peeking over her shoulder at me now and then. She had much longer hair, easily three times longer than her mother's, and it was kind of this matted, brown and cream coloration.

Just to the right of the shy female was an even younger one that was a little boy, and that little boy seemed to be the same height as me at the time and kept leaning out into the gateway so I got to see a lot of his body. He would lean out in an excited way and wave his hand at me and wave me over like *Come play with me, come play with me!*

To the other side of the mother was the father, who stood there looking very serious and very proud, like he would stick his chest out and look very dominant, like *I'm the big male around here.* I remember hearing other voices farther up in the forest, so I knew there were more here than what I could see, but these were the ones presenting themselves to me in a line like a family photograph.

I could see there was something else moving behind the hedge. I could just make out movement, but I couldn't see what it was. It was making me really nervous. The mother was trying everything she could to get my eyes on her and to show me that kind, loving, motherly face, to take all my anxiety away and make me come over and play. And the little boy really wanted me to. And then, they all realized what I was looking at, and the mother nudged the father, and he knelt down and yanked up this teenager that had been hiding behind the hedge. So he was made to stand next to the father, and he was almost as tall as the father, but he was a bit skinnier.

Now from left to right, I had this tall lanky one — he looked to be maybe eighteen in human terms — then the father, then the mother, then the girl, then the little five-year-old boy. And I just stood there in the middle of the field, and I could hear the mother's voice in my head. She was telling me, "It's okay, we're not going to harm you. You can come into the woods here and meet us." I remember saying back in my own mind's voice, "Where did you come from? How did you get here?" And just like at the bedroom window, my head got filled with all of these images of different woodlands and different rivers, and how they follow the rivers and use the woods. They painted this whole picture in my head of how they move across the landscape, and it was amazing. The mother told me that this was just a small part of their yearly travel route. She explained that this forest up here was a meet-up place for an extended tribe with multiple families all here at once.

I kept looking over my shoulder, back down the hill. This was just out of sight of the row of cottages. I kept thinking, *My mum lives down there.* I had this feeling like if I went with them I was never going home again. It was like a fork in the road. Do I stay with my human mum or do I get adopted by a family of Bigfoot.

Part of the fear was that I could hear others farther up in the woods that were doing loud whoops and calls. The other thing was that the one that had been hiding behind the hedge at first kept giving me a really evil look, like a grumpy teenager with a chip on his shoulder. I tried to tell the mother, "The second you turn your back on me he's going to pick on me." They were all looking really grumpy towards that son like he was messing everything up.

She felt saddened and let me go. She realized how scared I was. It felt like they weren't going to push it, and they just allowed me to run away. I remember just turning around and running away.

I ran home, and the first thing I told my mum was that there were really big hairy people in the woods, and she just thought they were lumberjacks. It wasn't till years later that the Patterson/Gimlin footage came on, and I remember pointing at the TV and shouting, "That's what I saw in the woods, Mum! That's what I saw!"

You hear these people that try to paint Bigfoot as something that would have killed me, eaten me or kidnapped me, but I didn't get any of those vibes from them whatsoever. They were like humans. If anything, I got a strong sense of intelligence, warmth, kind hearts, a sense of pride from the father definitely, but he wouldn't have harmed a hair on my head. I could tell that from him. He was a very honorable man. Part of their psychic ability seems to be that they can give you their entire character profile. Who they feel they are gets sent to your mind in one complete package as if you've known them for years.

That was the one and only time I'd had voices and images in my head. But I did have other encounters. Once, I was getting a lift from my mum, about five miles down the road to a little village, and we were going through these valleys, and I looked up one of the valleys and could see what looked like a male Bigfoot walking up a pathway, straight up the side of the mountain, and it just looked like a huge silverback gorilla walking on two feet up this path. You could just tell the size of the shoulders. It was in broad daylight, so you could see the shine of its black hair on its back and shoulders.

Another day, I was playing with three friends on this little woodland hill, and we were convinced that there were other kids in the woods with us that were playing tricks on us and throwing rocks at us. We figured out the trajectory of some of these rocks and sticks, and we knew they were coming from behind a certain bush, so were like, "Two of you go that way, two of us will go this way. We'll surround them." So we made our charge at this bush and tried to surround whatever was behind it, and my friend and I both got a glimpse of what it was, and it was another of these teenage male ones that are quite skinny and not very tall yet. I just remember the look of sheer shock on its face. It just turned around and fled with arms flailing like a cartoon. It just tore through loads of bushes, making a hell of a racket.*

---

*Sophie continues to interact with her local group, but these experiences no longer involve mindspeak.

6. Wayne and Todd: Alaska, Michigan

These brothers grew up in Alaska. Fifteen years ago, Wayne moved to Michigan, where his interactions began in earnest. Their account broadens the mindspeak experience to include a strong connection between two members of our own species, bonded since childhood, and members of the Sasquatch species. Moreover, the great distance between the brothers, once Wayne moved five thousand miles away, evidently has not raised any impediment whatsoever. We will revisit this concept in Part 4 in the discussion of quantum non-locality.

Wayne

So this whole Bigfoot thing...I'd always entertained the thought but never knew if they were real. I had a hard time with it because I grew up in the woods, long-line trapping. We were trappers for a living, so I thought if they were there, I was the one guy that should know about it. But I did see a track in 1978 on a mud bank on a creek about five miles from the road. It was a real small track and not a black bear. It looked almost human yet it didn't. And there's no reason a little tiny…it looked like maybe a three- or four-year-old kid would be out here in the middle of nowhere. So that was always in the back of my mind.

About twenty-five years later, I'm moose hunting. Now I'm fifty-two years old. I'm alone and I'm in the woods and I'm calling moose, and all of a sudden from upslope of me, I hear this commotion, and I look up the hill. I don't see anything, but I hear this thunderous footbeat on the ground, just rapid stomping, and it's coming down through the woods toward me. To say that I could hear it isn't enough. I could feel it through my whole body, reverberating. I'd never experienced anything like that.

So it's coming and it's coming very fast, and it's coming straight at me. But I can't see anything. I don't see any brush moving, although my ears are telling me it's literally thirty feet away. I pull my sidearm, and as soon as I do, the stomping stops right in front of me.

Then something went — and I can't do it justice because it was a much deeper voice — "Wwuup wwuup wwuup druh" right in front of me. Now I don't know if that was mindspeak. I don't know what happened. And to this day I cannot explain it, and I think about this every day of my life. I wish I'd been able to see it.

So that happens, and I go home and tell my wife, and my head is absolutely just spinning, trying to put the pieces together to make this work in my mind. You can't hear something that's not there.

A few years later, I was lying in bed one morning, awake. All of a sudden, *inside my head*, I start hearing this moaning and wailing. It just sounded like agony. At first I thought it was nearby and that I was hearing it through my ears. But then, I started to realize this was something different. And you couldn't make it stop or turn it down.

I got up and I asked my wife — she was in the living room — "Did you just hear that?" And she said no, what did I hear? I said, "I heard this wailing and moaning, and I think it was coming from inside my *head*."

And she said, "*What?*" It was the weirdest thing. I couldn't turn it off. It actually crossed my mind that I might be having an aneurysm. And just then, literally, like ten seconds later, the phone rings, and it's my brother in Michigan (I'm in Alaska), and he is just frantic on the phone.

Todd

My wife and I were driving home from the grocery store, and the closer we got to the house, the more I heard this wailing and moaning sound. I'd heard yelling, screaming, and other vocalizations near my property in Michigan, but never this sound. So we got closer and closer to the house from the store — we live in the country — and it kept getting louder. And I asked my wife, "Can't you hear that?"

She said, "I can't hear anything."

And I said, "Honey, I can hear moaning and wailing. It's driving me crazy."

Well, by the time we got into the driveway and got out of the car and took the food in, the noise was almost to the point of physically controlling me. I mean, not only could I hear it, but it was making my bones rattle. There was a sense of losing control of your senses, and it was so intense that I called Todd, and I said, "Something is horribly wrong." I said, "I don't know what it is, but I can't stop this sound. It's going to bring me to tears." I got definite *pain* from this.

I was going out into my woods, trying to figure out if that would help or if I'd find something wounded.

After he let me tell my story, Wayne said, "Todd, I just heard the same thing." Now remember, we're five thousand miles apart. That was the only time we experienced this kind of simultaneous psychic event.

Wayne

For the past three years, I've had the privilege of being allowed to interact with these things, and I've had more than my fair share of encounters, and I've always wondered, *Why us, why him and I?* When this all started to escalate, about three years ago, we were having activity at the house, but I didn't know how to address it. You know, I'd have stuff moved in the yard, stuff thrown. I was hearing screams, hollers, grunts, wood knocks, foot stomps. I found prints. The whole gamut. I haven't actually found many structures on my twenty acres of woods, but there's one big one near the house.

One night, Todd said, "Why don't you just try talking to them, through your mind or out in the open, just verbally out in the open?"

So I went out on the porch at night, and I started talking to them, and when I did that, my whole life changed forever. The communication floodgate was opened, because as soon as I started speaking, you know, "Whoever's out there, it's all right, you can talk to me," I heard one word repeated in my head: "Female. Female. Female. Female. Female…"

I said, "'Female,' okay, I get it." It was both an impression and a voice. And I got on the phone with Todd and I said, "Todd, it worked."

Two nights later, I heard a name, and it was "Falusha," and I thought, *What the hell? Who can dream this shit up?* I got some help to understand this from a person I was introduced to, a psychic channeler, and she helped me come to grips with what was going on. She said I was being contacted. I said, "Why me? Why us?"

"You have to be good of heart."

So it just progressed from there. We got past the introductions with the "female" thing in my head, then the first name came. And then, about a week later, a second name came, "Salamon," another female name. And I thought, *Oh, my God.*

And I was still having stuff moved around in the yard, and hearing the screams and everything. Then, one morning I was sitting at the house, getting ready to go to work. My wife was there and my grandson was there, and he wasn't quite two years old. And for some reason, just out of the blue, I got up out of the chair, threw on my shoes, and walked outside behind the garage. Lo and behold, there sat a female about forty feet away, sitting on a log. I wasn't scared. I wasn't nervous. I think they help calm you down mentally first. Prepare you.

Behind her, I could see this massive black shadow partly hiding behind a tree, like something that wouldn't quite come into focus for me, if that makes any sense.

And she was just sitting there. Sandy brown with a black face. Sandy brown from head to foot except for her face. Black eyes. No whites, no white in the eyes at all. She wasn't as big as you would think, maybe six feet if she'd stood up, but she didn't stand up. She raised an arm, and I knew that she wanted me to come out there in the woods.

I walked by them, probably ten feet away, and they never moved. They just looked at me, and I saw the female as clear as day. The shadow figure behind the tree never would come into focus. As I walked by them, I looked down at the ground, and I saw symbols. It was two symbols that just repeated themselves, one after the other, and they went on in a trail for God knows how long. They were images, *neon* images, laid out in a pathway.

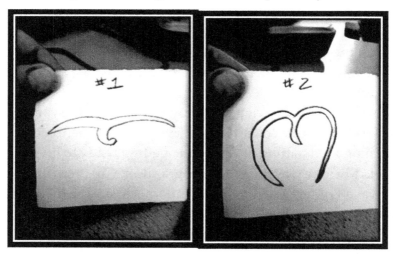

I looked down and I was like, *What in the hell is going on?* I didn't follow the pathway. I drew them right after, but to this day I don't know what they meant. When I turned back around, the two Sasquatch were gone. There was no evidence of them even being there because I looked everywhere.

Here's another incident. I had just opened the garage one morning and I got this imprint in my mind. It was just like a slide projector, this image. I saw a *wound* bleeding on an arm or a leg. I could see black hair with brownish hair mixed in. The image repeated itself, and I stood there just frozen.   I thought, *Something's wrong, something has happened.*

So I contacted my friend [the psychic channeler], and she said that one had been shot in the leg.

They contact you on their terms, through images, words, or phrases. Like if they want you to come outside, they'll just say, "Outside." I get up early and I'm usually up and on my front porch by five o'clock with a cup of coffee. And there's a lot of times that I've started to go outside, and the minute my foot hits the porch I'll hear the word, "In." So I go back inside. I just wait till it's light or it just feels like it's right to go back out. Maybe they do this 5% or 10% of the time. Obviously, there's something going on out there that they don't want me to hear or see. It can be dark or not, it doesn't really matter. It's all about their schedule.

They'll say, "Woods," and I'll go over to the woods. I never see anything except that one time with the symbols on the ground, but I never hesitate in doing what they ask me to do. I don't want to make it seem like it's a physical control, though. It's an intentional movement on my part to let them understand that *I* understand what they are saying to me. I think it's one big inspection. Trust is a really big thing with them, and I don't want to betray that. I'm still a little confused about why they chose me and my brother.

There's been a lot that goes on, but it doesn't go on continuously. It breaks. There was a break one time of six months without any activity at all, and then boom, it flooded again. I don't know where they go, but they obviously go somewhere. Once I start finding stuff that's been moved or rearranged at the house, I'll know. Then I'll start talking to them again. I'll say, "Good morning" or say their names.

Todd

One more thing I wanted to share from here in Alaska. I'd been interacting with them through objects at the gifting log nonstop at the same time every day, the same pattern. Then, I hurt my back and couldn't even get off the floor for four or five days. I'd ruptured some discs. One afternoon, I'm lying on the floor and this woman [the psychic channeler] calls and she's just frantic. She wants to know what's the matter with me, what's wrong? I was hurt and had to get to a doctor. She hadn't spoken with Wayne. She said, "They're telling me you're hurt."

I said, "Who's telling you?"

She said, "The Sasquatch. They know you're hurt." Then, she went on to describe my house to a tee, down to the twenty-four-foot trailer parked outside.

I'd mostly interact with them at the gifting log, but several times here at the house, I'd be outside at night working, and I could hear them in the brush. I would hear grunts or soft wood knocks or real low-key whoops. But I never knew they *cared* about me enough to communicate through that woman back to me. I guess I wasn't capable of mindspeak myself.

UPDATE: On February 21, 2019, Todd wrote me that the night before, very near his gifting log, amid multiple wood knocks, he found and photographed a trackway consisting of more than one hundred impressions in the snow.

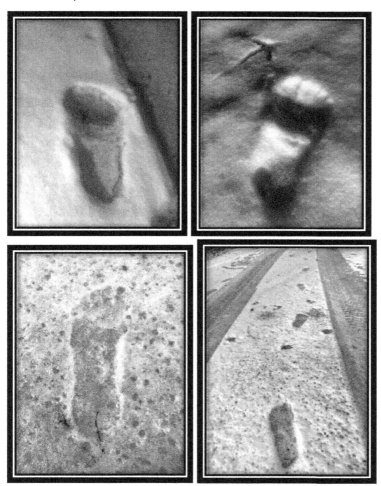

The next morning, he documented further. Stride length: 47 inches.

7. Connie Willis: Oklahoma

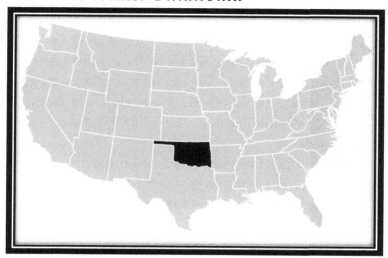

Ms. Willis shared this testimonial on her YouTube show "Blue Rock Talk," Oct. 5, 2018. Pay special attention to the careful way she explains the mindspeak experience — how it can sound at first like an ordinary, external voice, and then you recognize the difference.

I didn't hear it with my ears. But when you hear it, you don't think, *I didn't hear that with my ears*. You just get the message. It's as though you heard it, but you don't notice that it wasn't audible. It's *there*. That's what's crazy. You don't notice the difference until later when you realize, *Oh, that was not audible, but I just had a conversation*.

Sometimes, it's a full sentence, and you receive every word. But there have been other times where it's a message, and you just get the message, but not the words.

I'll give you an example. Friends took me to this place in Oklahoma, my first time ever going to an active spot. To a lot of them, this was old hat; they'd done this for years and years. We were settling in for the night and I got a message. You don't notice it at the time because it's so natural. It's not like the heavens open up and the waters part. It's not like that at all. It just happens, and you go with it. The message I got was that they were highly advanced, and they were everywhere. It was a *knowing*. You know when you suddenly know that you know something? It was just like that. *They're highly advanced and they're everywhere.*

And when I got this message, I had the sense I was being stared at from a certain spot, but I didn't know if it was true. Later, in the tent, I got the message, "Unzip this and look out. You'll see me."

And I was like, "No, no, I'm not ready for it."

"Well, this is what you came for, isn't it? "

That wasn't an inner voice of my own making. It even had *attitude*, and I was like, "Well, yeah, you're right, but I'm not ready for it. I just got here. It's my first night. I didn't expect anything."

They let me go. It was just like I was released from the thought. It was okay. They weren't going to argue it.

The next night, I was in a vehicle while everyone else stayed in the woods. We had had so much action that night, I was worn out. It was just too much. I'm like, *Oh my gosh, they exist, they're real, they talk*. And I sat in this vehicle while other people went to check something out. I'd had enough, and I couldn't decide if I wanted the vehicle on or off. *Is it going to be a beacon if it's on, and they come to me, and I'm alone in the car while everybody else is gone? Is it better to keep it off so it's quiet, and then they just walk right up to me and look through the window like in some of the documentaries where people have been witnesses to that and they're scared to death?*

As I was figuring out what to do, I just stopped and thought about the people down in the field, and I said to myself, "I wonder why they hide from us. I wonder why they *hide*."

And I heard, "Because our face frightens you, and that makes us sad."

I'm like "What?! I didn't think that thought." So they had feelings. They cared about mine, and they expressed theirs. Highly advanced.

8. Les Stroud: Tennessee

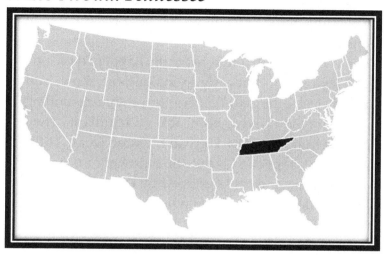

Mr. Stroud shared this testimonial on Episode 500 of Sasquatch Chronicles with Wes Germer. Like many mindspeak receivers, he initially lacked an appropriate frame of reference and assumed he must be going insane.

I was filming the "Smoky Mountain Bigfoot" episode of "Survivorman: Bigfoot" and I was with researcher Scott Carpenter. He took me out to his "hotspot," as we call them. I said, "Here's what I want to do. Just leave me out here, and you leave, and I'll stay out here until it gets dark. Everyone knows that's the creepiest time to be out in the forest…as it gets dark. And, of course, it was a stormy night, so the wind was blowing. I sat out there alone in his favorite spot where he has most of his encounters.

I thought, *Okay, I'm going to walk back in the dark now.* I was literally trying to tempt fate. If you watch the show, you see me say, "You know what, the hair just went up on the back of my neck. Let's just see what happens." So I'm like taunting the situation. Then we cut to commercial and when we came back, I just moved on because apparently nothing much happened.

That's not the truth, but what really happened I wasn't ready to share. Not that early in making the show, and why not? Because the gate-keepers [the producers funding the show] wouldn't have been able to handle it. They would have said, "No, Les, you can't...woah woah, TMI!"

Well, what happened was...the hair went up on the back of my neck, and I was gripped by this whole...hell, I've been stalked by a mountain lion and we ended up staring at each other fifteen feet away. So I understand wildlife well, but I don't get that fear factor. So there I am, in the dark, Smoky Mountains, and all my Neanderthal instincts are on high alert. And then...it hit.

I had never experienced this before in my life. It was like it was right in the middle of my head, right *inside* my brain. The strongest-ever voice that was not my own. It just said, "If you want to meet us, stay the night."

And I just stood there gripped in fear. I was like stammering. I felt that there was something standing right over there on that hill. There was a gully and then a hill, and it felt that it was a big, prime-of-his-life male and a smaller young one. And then the voice said, "We're over here on the hill. But you have to stay."

I thought, *I gotta answer*. And in my voice, in my brain, I just said, "I'm not ready for this. I can't."

And then it was literally, "Okay." And it turned and walked away. The feeling went away. The hairs went down on the back of my neck. It was gone, it was over.

It was so weird that went I got home I actually went and talked to a counselor and said, "Listen, what's schizophrenia?"

She said, "First of all, if you had schizophrenia, you wouldn't be asking me." So it was the weirdest thing ever.

Now since then, I've experienced mindspeak three other times. By now I take it kind of casually, because I thought: It's just telepathy. A lot of people talk about it. Scientists study telepathy. Maybe that's an attribute of the Sasquatch species because they don't have our larynx and our vocal chords. Maybe that's their language. Maybe they're born with a strong capacity. What if we are all born with the ability to use telepathic communication?

9. Stewart: Oklahoma

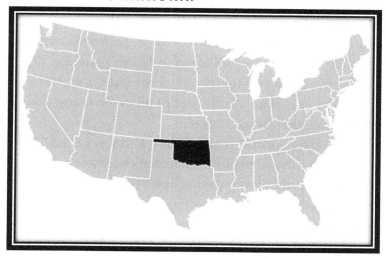

This interview is posted on the North American Bigfoot Search website, Nabigfootsearch.com, Report #63, Investigator: Richard Hucklebridge. Stewart is one of those fortunate few who are able to tap into this level of communication right away. His experience also resonates with those of others — Denise, Connie, Sophie, Todd, etc. — who have found themselves faced with one or more Sasquatch, either as a mental image or as a real-world manifestation, as though our next of kin are introducing themselves to us.

In mid-April, 2011, a Native American drum-making workshop was being hosted on private land that was located along a tributary creek feeding into Xxxxxx Lake, Oklahoma. I had recently met and conversed with the land owner at a Sasquatch conference. She had had regular interactions with her friends, "The Forest People." She even referred to some of them by name, which at the time sounded far too incredible for me. On the other hand, I perceived her to be very honest, open and sincere in sharing her experiences with no hidden agenda.

My perceptions at that time were that these subjects were nothing more than an undiscovered primate animal lurking about in the wooded areas of North America. I'd jumped at the chance to travel out to her land. I wasn't a bit interested in making drums but planned on using this time to explore this remote forest.

I arrived at the location early Friday, February 15, 2011. The elevation is about six hundred feet above sea level and has rolling, heavily wooded hills and creek valleys. The weather was cool, partly to mostly clear with day temperatures reaching into the high 50s and then dropping down to the low 40s at night. A sustained southeast wind blew most of the time we were there.

The group that attended the workshop numbered about twenty-five. A number of them were of full- or mixed-blood Native American lineage. The Sasquatch subject was not a focus of the gathering and was not openly discussed much. I paid for the food and lodging portion of the costs and then hung out in the surrounding woods during the daytime workshop activities. The host had no problem with this but stipulated that I not reveal any specific locations of this land to any third party.

I spent the better part of two days hiding out in the woods by myself. I heard various calls, wood knocks, and movement, but had no sightings. Something was definitely moving about out there but keeping a good safe distance.

On the workshop lunch break of the second day, four ladies from the group went out on a short hike on the north side of the property. They came back less than an hour later gushing about how they had just seen a Bigfoot peeking at them from behind a tree. I was a bit envious, having spent much more time than them out in the woods.

On a later break, I talked two of these ladies into taking me back to the precise location where they'd seen the Bigfoot. On reaching this location, we waited and scanned the area. In a few short minutes, we could hear heavy movement in the brush about one hundred yards down the hill towards the creek.

I took out my pocket mini-cam and began scanning the area. I captured a subject peering back at us from about 150 yards away. It wasn't an animal, moved like a human. I have since downloaded it to YouTube under the title "Young Bigfoot Caught Peeking." He looks very human at some angles, very different at others. The video is shaky and distorted, but still amazing.

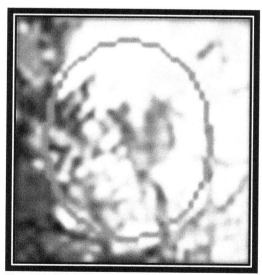

Two-thirds profile, mouth open.

I was happy to have seen something at a distance but still wanted to see one of these elusive subjects much closer. Later that evening, I was back in the woods by myself. I sensed they were close and watching. Becoming a bit frustrated, I began to reach out to them in a very direct manner.

"I just want to clearly see you!" I spoke out facing the dense section of woods. This action was very significant to what happened later that night. No one from the group was even close to me out here. This was to be the start of my change of thinking, as to who and what was living out in the woods. I would soon learn they are much like us in some ways and very different in others.

"I will not hurt you or reveal your location to another," I continued.

Later that evening, a scheduled fireside service began with wooden flute music, drum beating, chanting, and dancing. After participating in several ceremonies, I eased away from the group, moving well out of sight in the dark, then flanking back towards the opposite side of the gathering. I was doing this to ensure that someone from the group would not know exactly where I was. I wasn't expecting any tricks or pranks from the folks here, but at the same time, I was making provisions to ensure that this kind of stupid nonsense wouldn't easily happen without very coordinated and focused efforts.

I had spent several hours out there in the brush, scanning with my night vision scope. The time was now well past midnight. I was watching the tree line bordering the adjacent meadow, hoping to see and video any movement. Suddenly, a figure moved out of the tree line and into the meadow back on the north side. I began to video it but soon realized it was the land owner/host. What caught my attention was that she was not walking back towards the fireside gathering but instead coming straight towards my hidden location several hundred yards to the south.

She never wavered and walked right up to me.

"How did you know I was here!?"

"The Forest People told me where you were and that I should come and get you" was her reply. I was astonished, yet still cautious about being set up. If this was a setup, those participating in it would have had to have excellent night vision capabilities.

"Would you like to go see them?" she continued. At this point, I knew this was not mere coincidence. Her finding me and these words sealed it. Someone or something had heard and understood my query earlier today. Now, whether it was still a prank, or for real, I gave her a firm yes.

"One rule is that you do not use any lights or cameras unless you ask me first," she instructed. "They do not like these items that are held up to your face, is that clear?" I agreed, and we began walking back north, still a distance from the group.

We moved beyond the fenced-in pasture and paused by the closed cattle gate. The host then began to call out, using several names I do not recall. Immediately, I began to hear heavy footfalls moving through the thick brush towards us. They started several hundred yards due east and steadily moved through the heavy underbrush toward us. Another set began approaching from the northeast, and then a third set to our south.

This was very thick Oklahoma woods that I would have difficulty moving through in the daytime. I saw no lights whatsoever but could clearly hear the steady movement coming closer. I was still vaguely skeptical, but anyone going through this much trouble for a simple prank, pushing through the remote woods at night, would have to be nearly insane or very desperate and get very little personal gain in return.

At some point, I began to feel this overwhelming presence and the sensation of being watched as the steps moved to within about twenty feet of the tree line and stopped. It was a similar feeling to being surrounded by a high-tension, static electrical field, which makes your hair stand up on end. A very pronounced feeling and presence that is difficult to explain but real nonetheless.

I was now sure something besides a few pranksters was out there in the brush and asked my host if I could use my night vision scope to possibly view them. She said yes, and I turned on the scope, but it wouldn't work. I recycled the switch and it still didn't work. I was freaking out at this turn of events because it was a brand new item and I'd had no trouble with it the two previous nights.

"It won't work," I told her. She just smiled back at me and told me to try it now. It turned on and was working fine. This was very hard for me to fully comprehend, but I knew for sure that a few jokers in the brush could not have caused this anomaly.

The scope was not a FLIR (thermal-imaging device) and could not penetrate far into the brush. I couldn't see a thing but could feel something was out there very close and intently watching us. The growing anxiety of the unknown gripped me. I don't do vulnerable very well, and

I was now beginning to feel very overwhelmed. Something I didn't understand was unfolding and the only trust I now had was in the host's extremely calm demeanor.

"Would you like to go inside there and see them?" she asked. If the host had been a man, I would have probably declined at this point, but my testosterone pride just would not let me wimp out in front of a woman. I replied with a somewhat tentative yes, thinking, *What am I getting myself into?*, and we moved through the gate and down the brush line for about a hundred feet.

The trail went off into the woods. I was right behind the host, following her in the direct moonlight. Once inside the dark canopy with lesser light, I could barely see her and followed very, very closely behind her. I could hear stirring and movements all around us in the brush but was afraid to look, keeping my eyes on the host's dim form moving in front of me. There was the crushing of leaves and the stirring branches all around us, but I kept my eyes forward, staying close, knowing the host was their friend and my security blanket at this point.

I felt totally wide open and completely exposed. I was in the middle of their house now and couldn't see them. This was not in my comfort zone at all!

We turned off the main trail at about a hudred yards distance and onto an intersecting path. We moved about fifty feet down it and came to a clearing that was about twenty feet in diameter. It had two metal folding chairs sitting in the middle. This was the place she'd meet the Forest People. It was a place that, she said, she had rarely brought a visitor to. This was a direct response to their specific instructions to her.

We stopped, and she began to speak out to them again. I stood close beside her and could now see dark shapes moving about but nothing clearly because of the low light conditions. Something happened to me at this point that is very difficult to fully explain unless a person has specifically encountered it, but it happened to me nonetheless.

Very clearly in my head (not with my ears) I heard the words, "Why are you carrying a gun?" I was shocked at this very distinct question. No one here at the get-together knew I was carrying a 45 ACP discreetly tucked away on my person. It is a habit many from active and retired law enforcement legally stick to, and no one will ever see or know it is there.

I was stunned at this chain of events and thought I just might be imagining these words. Then, they came back to me about ten times stronger in my head: "WHY ARE YOU CARRYING A GUN!?" I had no doubt it was the Forest People talking directly to me.

I also can't explain how I knew how to reply to the voice. Maybe it is a deeply hidden primal instinct we have used in our past and is now a lost art. Somewhere in my head I replied, "It is a tool of protection I have carried on my job. I carry it around my close friends and family. I have never hurt them with it, and I will not hurt you now."

Immediately after my answer, the voice in my head specifically named my host and told me to step away from her. I looked back at the land owner and told her, "They are telling me to step away from you."

She didn't look one bit surprised at my words and smiled back at me. "Do what they say…"

I have faced many unique and dangerous situations in my life, most in my first public safety career, but nothing ranks even remotely close to the feelings I had at this point. I was close to something very powerful and living that I did not understand. It had reasoning and sensing abilities far beyond my understanding.

I felt like I was stepping off the edge of the Grand Canyon as I moved back away down the trail all by myself in the dark. This was certainly way out of my comfort zone and I only hoped and prayed for the Creator's divine protection over me at this point. "Whatever happens here, I am in Your hands, Lord…"

I walked back to the trail intersection and felt the impulse to stop here. I gazed to my left deeper down the trail. Suddenly, a tall figure stepped out from behind a tree about fifty feet away. It was like Ed Sullivan used to do on his show, stepping out from behind a curtain. The figure moved from the tree and right into a beam of moonlight filtering down through the overhead foliage canopy.

This guy was massive! He was about ten feet tall with super-broad shoulders, domed head, and covered with long hair. He was at least eight hundred pounds. I could clearly see his face intently watching me. He held his position in the light and began slowly swaying from side to side, still watching me.

"Can you see him?" my host asked. She had followed at a short distance.

"Yes, I can see him, and he is swaying from side to side."

"Sway with him."

I have no idea what the significance of this swaying was, but when I started to do this another Bigfoot rose out of the brush no more than twenty feet in front of me. He was not much taller than my six-foot stature but considerably thicker and hair covered. I could see his face, which had the expression of total amazement. His eyes were wide and his jaw hung open as we both looked at each other. Then he silently turned back and looked at the big one, then back to me, doing this several times. The lower half of his body was hidden by the thick brush he rose up out of.

He looked like something right out of a Stephen Spielberg movie, yet alive and breathing no more than twenty feet away.

At this time, one about eight feet tall stepped out in front of the taller one, then another one stepped out onto the trail directly in front of me. I don't know how I knew this, but she was a young female and also about six feet tall. At her feet, I could see a toddler scampering around that was about two and a half to three feet tall. Being a parent, this hit me like a ton of bricks. I realized the Bigfoot were trusting me enough to allow their young to draw very close and get a real good look.

All my apprehension suddenly vanished, and I became very relaxed, actually laughing and giggling at this truly amazing encounter. I saw the toddler finally look up and notice me. It paused and watched me, then all at once, ran towards me with both of its arms pointed up ready to be picked up.

My heart skipped a few beats. This hairy little child was moving towards me wanting to be innocently picked up. Now, I could stand being close to these subjects, but I am certain my heart could not have taken it if this completely foreign youngster had latched onto me!

Thank God, the young female lunged out and grabbed the baby by one arm and pulled it back to her. Fearing all that was happening was way too much for my already high blood pressure, I asked my host to lead me out of there.

At no time did I feel the Bigfoot were aggressive. They silently and very politely held their positions except for the toddler's action, which was totally unexpected.

I had been granted my wish and seen the Forest People up close. As we left, one further back broke out in a series of owl calls, which I was able to record on my mini-camcorder. It all seemed to happen very fast, yet the group later told us we were in there the better part of an hour.

I do not recall ever experiencing any bad odors or discomfort other than my initial fear and apprehension. The land owner does have a good, trusting relationship with this particular clan. She is extremely guarded as to who she shares this information with and rightfully so.

10. Ann: Minnesota

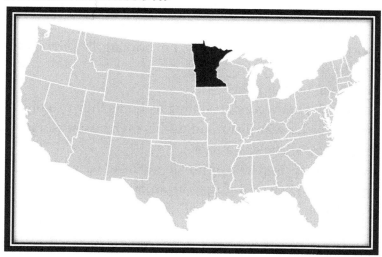

Ann's account represents the mild end of the spectrum; she has received subtle impressions rather than explicit messages or voices.

We have this house in northern Minnesota. I had a job in central Minnesota. I would commute back and forth but be home up here on weekends. One Sunday night in October, 2007, it was raining and cold and it's one of those rains where it just eats up the light, and the main highway heading south from near our place had just been re-blacktopped. I was still not too far from our house and driving kind of slow because we're in deer country, and I didn't want to hit one.

All of a sudden, this tall, red-haired guy runs across the road in front of me in like two leaps. He was a lean guy with fur all over — well, not fur, more like hair because even though it was wet, it would blow as he moved. And he apparently didn't know I was coming either because he had the most startled look on his face. He was as surprised as I was, and I remember hearing a thought: "Oh no, I didn't know a car was coming!"

And I told him, "Don't worry, I'm braking, I'm *braking*, I won't hurt you."

And then he was gone.

My headlights were not shining as far as they usually do, so maybe he was just minding his own business. He might have been chasing a deer.

I wasn't surprised to hear him in my head because I've had horses, and I've grown up with animals — dogs, cats — and you get so you kind of...I don't know if it's anticipation or intuition. There's a way of knowing what they're thinking. I've been listening to wildlife all my life because I grew up in the woods, walking around in the woods, hearing the animals, hearing the trees, hearing even the little plants on the ground.

The next thing that happened was in spring, 2012. I'm in my kitchen. I don't know if I was washing dishes or making some stew. We've got these big, floor-to-ceiling, plate-glass windows overlooking the yard. We've got a little shack out there, and I've got a garden out there. So I just happen to glance up, see the shack, see a weird lump by the corner. I'm going, *What the hell is that, a raccoon sitting on it?* So then I really looked at it, and no, it was a big brown *face*. Someone standing behind the corner of the shack, looking through the window at *me* in my *kitchen*. And I'm going, *Oh..my...gosh*. And now I'm thinking, *So there's more than one of them around here*. The first guy I saw was tall and lean and red haired. This new guy was stockier and broader with a rounder face and definitely different features. I mean, they didn't even look like they were related. I'm thinking, *Okay, these forest people, there might be a whole tribe of them around.*

But this guy. He didn't seem threatening at all. He was just watching, and I could tell he was thinking, *What is that lady in there doing?* I wouldn't say it was really mind*speak.* It's not like words. It's just a sudden thought, like *This fellow's just watching me and he doesn't mean any harm.* How would I know he means no harm?

After I saw his head, he turned around and just walked away. I saw a portion of his shoulder and arm and leg on one side. He kind of used the shack as cover between me and him when he walked away, but I did see one side of the rest of him, and he was kind of shaking his head like we would do: *I can't figure it out.*

Later, I measured the roof there and figured out that he was about seven and half feet tall.

Then, in the summer of 2012, I was out in my garden weeding. It's just on the west side of the house, and it goes up a slope facing southwest, and there's a rock wall, and we kind of have a trail around the backside of the rock wall, and we've left some stumps standing up, about three or four feet tall, and they've got bunches of hazel bush and chokecherry that grow around them because they must like to grow where the roots of the stumps are rotting.

Anyway, I'm weeding my garden, and all of a sudden, something made me look up, and I'm going, *What is that back there?* I walk to the top of the slope. I look over the rock wall, and here's like a red-haired teenage girl crouching on the ground, hoping I'm thinking she's a stump too, only I say, "I *do* see you." Then, she got up, and she had this very chagrined look on her face, and she just turned around and walked away.

In saying she was a teenage girl, I'm kind of just doing mental extrapolation between our species of human development and what I saw of the two guys before. She looked only partially developed, and she was only about five feet tall, not even as tall as me. And I kind of got the thought that Mom had told her to go out foraging. I've got all those nice chokecherries growing back there. Plus, there's a raspberry patch. And here I was out in the yard, so she felt she had to hide, but then I saw her so she decided, *Well, there's no point in hiding anymore. May as well go back.* But I got the idea from her that she had to practice being elusive more. She's just a kid and needs to work on Bigfoot skills.

I guess I'd say I'm just more of a receiver of thoughts, though I have gone out and said out loud, "I don't mean you any harm, and I'm not going to tell anybody about you." Sometimes, I go out in the yard and I see something out of place. Our yard is fenced in because we've got two dogs, a Malamute and a husky, and we don't want them running around for four hours or forty miles, whichever comes first, so one day, I walked this fence to make sure it was still good. Lots of times, a bear wants to get at the raspberries and will pop a fence post out and come across.

Anyway, so I'm tramping the trail along the fence, and I look out to this little ravine that's at the edge of our yard, just outside the fence, and I see a stump, and I'm going, *You know what, we don't have a stump there.* And then, Gray-Haired Grandpa gets up and runs off down the ravine.

When he saw me coming down the trail, he must have just crouched down in plain sight, pretending to be a stump, and he looked so much like a stump that if I hadn't known we didn't have a stump there because of the logging operations we do, I never would have given it a second glance.

For years, I worked at a large commercial landscape nursery, and my job was counting plants and knowing what plants were where. All that practice at my job lets me look at a forest of trees and bushes and plants and know every one of them and realize when something's out of place.

In 2013, we had a forest fire. It burned much of the state land to the far western edge of our property and county tax forfeit land that surrounds us. I didn't see a whole lot of visitors for a while, but they started to come back about 2016. They play silly tricks on me, like I leave my gardening tools outside and find them picked up and "put away" in weird places. I'll leave them in the garden and then they're over there by the Jack pine tree. I ask my husband, "Where did you put my shovel and rake and cultivators," and he goes, "I didn't put 'em anywhere."

11. John: California

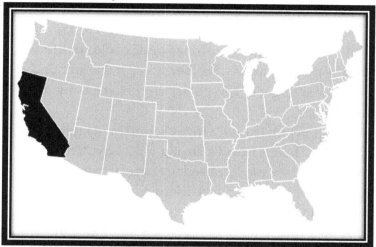

Here is an example of brief, pragmatic communication. On three occasions over ten years, John received messages that were crisp and to the point, fitting the particular situation at hand. Unlike others, he has not experienced any follow-up expansion of mindspeak, even though he has found himself in close proximity to Sasquatch five more times.

Sequoia Incident 1985

We had spent a long weekend cross-country skiing in amongst the giant redwood trees of Sequoia. It was beautiful and serene. Over that entire weekend, I had a feeling that we were being watched as we played around in the snow, yet I never saw a thing.

Late in the afternoon of the final day, we packed up the van and headed down the mountain. As we drove, I could have sworn I heard someone say, "We've been watching you." I was totally confused, and I thought, *Who is "we"?*

As we rolled further down the mountain and came around a bend, I looked up to the left, and about seventy feet away, and thirty feet up the embankment from the road, was a huge male Bigfoot with a gray beard and long hair. His face was dark, with deep-set eyes. He had stepped out of the edge of the forest and I could see his red eyes in the dusk light. My brother was driving my dad's van. I was sitting on the cooler in between my two brothers.

At that moment, I heard a fuzzy sound in my mind like an old radio, Then, I heard a strong voice say, "Don't tell your family you see me." I raised my hand to point at him, and as I did so, he turned and disappeared into the trees. I believe he revealed himself to me on purpose, but I broke the trust by trying to point him out. I remember that I did not say a thing to anyone in the van, thinking, *They wouldn't believe me anyway.*

The whole mindspeak thing freaked me out and I think I was in denial for quite some time. Later on, I realized that this kind of psychic communication had happened before.

Kerm River Incident 1982
We were backpacking deep in the Sierras. One night around midnight, I heard something shifting large boulders in a nearby stream. A few hours later, I heard owl-like screeches and what sounded like a gibberish conversation in our camp. I felt my tent shaking and smelled the most god-awful sewer smell. I thought my brother had passed gas, but it was far worse than that. I distinctly remember the words "When will they leave?" popping into my mind, and I somehow knew that that was the Bigfoot asking that question. They seemed to drift off

up the mountain and things settled down for a time. Around four, I remember there were pebbles being thrown at my tent, then more tent shaking. Then, I also distinctly remember someone palming my head through the tent. I thought it was my dad, so I pushed it away. The hand then slapped my head — not Dad. I then heard loud feet running away up the mountain.

Mendicino Incident 1975

I was visiting some family friends in Mendicino north of San Francisco. Their son, about my age, had built a tree house between three trees and about twenty feet up. It was down by the edge of the property. He asked if I wanted to camp overnight in the treehouse, and I said, "Sure." So we grabbed our sleeping bags and climbed up the ladder.

Sometime after midnight, I was awakened and noticed some glowing eyes and a face staring up at me, almost smiling, from the open transom near the top of the roof. First of all, we were twenty feet up and there was no way a person would be hanging on the outside of the treehouse. I thought it was my imagination, so I rolled over and tried to sleep again.

I was awakened again by a figure standing over both of us. Around this time, I became aware that I was being urinated on. I could hear someone making a kind of dry laugh. I reached out toward him and he began screaming and growling, and I could hear his toenails scratching against the plywood floor. I thought, This can't be real. He sounded exactly like the Ron Morhead recordings of the chimp-like sounds.

I spoke to it: "What are you?"

This only made him scream more. The mental message I received was, "Don't touch me or I will tear you apart."

At this point, my friend yelled at the animal and made sort of a lunging motion toward him. Since he was used to these animals, he knew it could be easily spooked. He turned toward the door and I felt the whole treehouse sway as he jumped the twenty feet to the ground. We could hear him crash through the trees with a long howl.

I asked, "Is he gone?"

My friend said, "Yes."

In the morning, I was convinced that it was some awful nightmare. When I asked my friend about what had happened, he said he didn't want to talk about it. I know it really happened because when we came back up to the house our parents were saying that we absolutely reeked of urine. Still, since I was only nine years old, it took me many years before I came to the only logical explanation — we'd had a very close encounter with a young male Bigfoot.

12. Paul: West Virginia, Pennsylvania

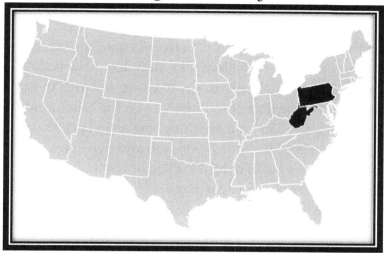

This testimonial appears on "Brenton Sawin Mysteries to Search," YouTube, August 16, 2016. I draw your attention to two features of his account: 1. In Paul's childhood communications with the juvenile female Sasquatch, he was not aware of her using mindspeak per se, though over time he realized that he'd never once caught her lips moving while she was "talking" to him; 2. His two experiences, in West Virginia and Pennsylvania, represent the two ends of the spectrum from kind and loving to fierce and vengeful – the second probably resulting from Paul's taking of a large fish from the adult male's territory.

Back in the early 1970s, my mom and dad had some issues. He was a biker, and she was a Christian. They collided. I ended up in a foster home in Cumberland, West Virginia. They had a summer camp on a lake. First summer I got there, I was six and solo, the only kid playing around here. I was permitted to go down to the docks and play in the lake as long as I had my arm floaties on and my vest. I would never drown, that's for sure.

Things started happening. Things would be moved out of place. My toys wouldn't be where I left them.

So one day I'm playing down at the docks, and I hear something from the row of pine trees behind me, saying not "yoo hoo" but something like that, like somebody's trying to get your attention. I walked up towards those pine trees. I remember standing there on the beach bank and looking. Couldn't see anything, so I went back to the dock and grabbed the little floaty raft, and two kids came out from those pine trees and walked down to the water, but they were not on the right-hand side of the dock where the houses were. They were on the left-hand side down in the cove area.

So I'm watching them and I'm like *Wow, there's something strange about them*. After watching them for a while, I decide to just go on down there, maybe just wave and get their attention. I was a shy kid. I wasn't bold enough to just go right up to them.

They were down at the water line. They were strange looking from a distance, but as I got closer they got more so. It was like a change happened from looking like humans to looking not so much. So I was cautious and a little nervous, but eventually we ended up sort of gathering together, and I ended up in the water myself on the edge there. I noticed that they were chasing all the little black catfish, the little babies, and eating them. That was our first encounter. I went back home.

In the next week or two, I saw them from a distance. One day, I was at the dock, they were at the pine tree line, and the girl came down to the dock. I was in my floaties feeling stupid, standing in the water. I'm not allowed to go past the end of the dock. She came into the water and we ended up splashing and playing around. She could swim. We swam. We started racing between the two docks, mine and the next one. I tried I don't know how many times. I even took my floaties off and tried beating her to the other dock. I ended up getting mad and getting up on the dock and crying. There was nothing I could do: You can run faster, jump farther, outswim me...

My foster parents had no clue, and that became an issue. I was sat down and questioned about who I was playing with. I said, "They're black, lotta hair, and they're naked." My foster dad says, "Oh, they're just black kids. They're poor. That's no big deal." I'd never seen a black person before, so I was like, "All right, wow, cool."

But the girl's not okay with meeting *them* at all. She's like, "That's not going to happen. Your parents and my parents...we're never going to be able to do that." She was just against it. I tried to explain but she was having trouble understanding that I had real parents and foster parents. I took a stick and drew a dad figure, then a mom figure, and then little me. I pointed and said, "This is me." And then over here I drew another female stick figure, with hair, and then a man. I said, "This is my real mom, this is my real dad, but they live over somewhere else." She didn't understand.

It was really crazy because you're sitting there and thoughts would pop in your head, like *bing*. She's talking, but are her lips moving? It seemed like she was always behind me when she talked. You'd look, and she'd just look back at you and smile. It's almost like she knew you had that thought in your mind. I felt like she knew my thoughts—*look at her hands..look at her feet..check her lips*— before I did.

I keep playing like I'm playing with other kids. But there are times when I'm looking and I'd see the feet and be like *Those feet are not like my feet*. Or I'd see their hands and their fingers were long and I'd be like *Your fingers and your hands are not like mine. I've got little stubby fingers*. There were pads on their hands, thick and dark.

She had a moon-pie-shaped head. Her hair was black. It was short. On her body, I'd say the hair kind of laid down. The first year when I met her, she was tubby. I didn't know it was a her. It was just an it. And the brother was just an it too. I didn't know any difference. One day, I think it was the day when he ate the mushroom, that's when I noticed that he had a penis. Not like a man's but long and thin. Then, I looked at her, and she had nothing, so then I knew.

She had short hair—maybe an inch long—all over her body, but it was thinner on her belly. Her face was like this Curious George mask outline, an ashy gray color, like an ape's face. I remember looking at her face and it was like it morphed in front of me. Sometimes, I'd look and it would be more ape-like, and then when she'd notice me looking and got my attention, it was more human. It was confusing and very strange. Maybe it was an inner thing just to keep myself calm.

He, the brother, didn't have the moon-pie-shaped head. You know how people describe their heads as conical? This was more of a slope. The hair tapered up.

The ears were not like ours. Well, they *kind* of were because they come out from the head a little bit, but more like a clamshell.

The palms of their hands and their feet were tough. Their fingers were long. Fingernails were dirty black. I do remember asking them several times, "Do you ever wash your *hands*?"

I used to play with my Super Soaker, and my foster mom put liquid soap in it to make bubbles. Well, the girl liked that thing. That was awesome. She looked at those bubbles and would follow them. Then one day, the Super Soaker's gone! Never did get it back.

I couldn't hang around the house and play with them, so they'd call me over to the woods, and I'd go over there and play with them.

One day, the brother comes along from out of the woods, and there were these mushrooms with these Japanese beetles all over them. So he's looking at one, and he looks over at her, and then he goes over and he hits the mushroom, knocks the beetles off, snatches the mushroom out of the ground and starts eating it. And I was like, "Oh, that's dirty, you should clean that first." He just looks at me. He never talked to me. I'd say things verbally to him, but there was nothing between us like me and her. He was just not into me, or I guess he was not into the whole thing, this interaction.

Another day, I got my butt beat by my dad, and I got smacked in the mouth by my foster mom because they said I was lying to them about my friend. They never grasped the idea of this being a reality. I'm having fun with my friend that I cannot prove to them, show them, introduce to them. It's like living in a parallel dimension.

I took walks with her. I even asked her one time, "Hey, where do your parents live?" And as we're walking out towards the point, out at the end of that inlet, she points off to the southwest and said, "Afar away that way." As far as I knew, there was nothing but woods in that direction. I just left it at that.

I'd come back from two hours of playing with her and my dad would say, "You smell like you fell in shit and rolled in trash." So I'd say to my foster mom and dad, "But I'm clean. There's no dirt. I didn't even sit down on the ground." She'd say, "You can't smell that?" I can hardly smell. One time I was sprayed by a skunk and couldn't even smell that. When I was three years old, my older sister was spinning me around and I slipped out of her hands, banked into the metal bedframe and broke my nose.

What was really strange was that whenever my foster parents started down the driveway, if I'd be playing with her, I'd go to turn around to say something to her, and I'd hear this noise, and she...I don't know...leaped like a frog? I don't know what she did really, but she went from A to B and disappeared that quick. And I was like *Where'd you go?* I'm looking around and can't see her anywhere.

On another occasion, she also leaped like this from down by the docks up into a pine tree, and my foster parents came walking down with their gear getting ready to jump in the lake and sunbathe, and she stayed right up there, and they walked by and didn't even know she was in that pine tree. She sat up there and watched us play for hours. And after they went back up, she came back down, and I was like "Wow. You could've met my foster parents." She was like, "That wouldn't work out. That's no good. That's not a good idea."

Another time, there was a winter storm, and my foster dad decided to go back up there to check the summer camp, and he took me with him. I decided to walk down to the lake. I was all geared up. I had these black rubber boots with these little snap cleat deals that lock up from the front, like five of them, so I snap them all closed and I'm walking through the snow. And I'm down there messing around, and the dock was pulled up out of the water and was sitting up on the beach next to the pine trees, and there was this big eye bolt there and I was just spinning it around in place, and I see her on the other side down at the cove in the tall grass.

I walk over to her, and we're playing and walking on the ice. She's the one who initiated it. There was a thin layer with water lapping against the beach, but this thick layer too that she was walking on. And there's this catfish underneath. She suddenly punched through the ice with her hand, grabbed the fish out, offered me part of it. It must have been a foot and a half long. It was a pretty big catfish. She just broke into it and was eating it and offered me part of it, and I was like "Oh no, you gotta cook that first."

They were perfectly suited to their environment. They knew what to eat and what to do. I remember this one time, she walked over to a pine tree and was grabbing some pine cones, and I don't know where she got it from, but she came back over with these great big yellow grub worms. I ate one with her, then I was just like "No, I don't think I should do that. I don't think that's a good idea." Especially when you crunch into that head.

I don't think you could have taken her anywhere else away from that environment. Everything was right there, and she knew everything. She knew everything to provide for herself. Like her brother too. He just smacked those beetles off that mushroom and ate it. They knew that area. After that, maybe they had to go somewhere else, going into preparations for going into adulthood.

The following summer is when I noticed she had changed. She was no more a chunky girl. She had thinned out and she just had small breasts coming out, maybe like a thirteen-year-old girl. And then I was like, "Oh, you need some clothes on." Every time that I said something that had to do with her presentation and her natural form, she distracted me. She would take me onto something else, ask me questions, take me off of it.

She let me know that they transform. "When we grow up, we change as far as how we respond to you." She was pushing this idea, like "Hey, you need to know that they [adults] are not the same as we [kids] are. When we grow older, this interaction is not acceptable anymore." I felt like this was not of their own free will, but it was like a forced thing. A transformation. And of course me, I was like, "Well no, my parents are fine with it. It's cool." And she's like, "No, they wouldn't be fine with me at all." That's how that went.

At the end of our time playing together, she told me, "I'll be leaving and going a long ways and won't be back...may not see you again." I remember being broken hearted. I started crying. I said, "No way." This was my best friend, you know? I've never really gotten over losing her.

A few years later, when I was twelve, in Pennsylvania, still with my foster parents, I used to go play by these woods in a part where men had come and taken the trees down. There was maybe a quarter mile of piles of just the treetops in rows. I'd go and play in these and climb all the stumps. There was a river and train tracks too.

One day, I was fishing there, and I tossed my lure in, a row of worms on the hook, and as I was walking down off the side of the bridge, the concrete framing, and dragging it along, I scored a fourteen-inch trout. I won the trophy for rainbow trout for Pennsylvania that season just by accident. The next weekend, I got my plaque with my trout on it, preserved, and I went back down there. I decided to take the backway home, which was the old railroad tracks. It had an old bridge — no tracks anymore, just the cross ties, and some of them were rotting or missing. It was always an adventure.

So I'm on my way back, and I thought, *Somebody's down here fishing*. It sounded like people talking, muffled, across the creek, but I never saw anybody. I was just walking along leisurely. I felt like somebody was watching me or following me, or maybe somebody was trying to taunt me. There were always these goofy older kids that ran around, the drinkers and the pot smokers…all these clowns doing something. So I just assumed it was that.

After half a mile, I really felt like something was on me, something was attached to me. I felt like the atmosphere around me was thick. I felt a background sense of fear coming on or trying to apply itself to me. So I'm looking around and crouching and bobbing and kneeling down and trying to see into the brush against the light from the other side to see if I could make out a figure. I was like, *Man, something's going on here.*

All of a sudden, voices come alive in my head — audible, loud voices, saying stuff like, "You need to get out of here. This is dangerous. There's something not right here. Keep going. Do not stop. You shouldn't be looking around." I'm really trying to figure it out because I'd always played here. It was right by our *town*. I had no fears. We'd ride our three-wheelers and dirt bikes up and down this road all the time.

So I kept challenging this feeling and kept looking all around me. The voices kept saying, "You need to go," and I'm thinking, *Go? Go where? What's wrong. Why am I having this intense push?* But as I'm resisting, it just gets thicker and the voices get louder, and I remember looking back to my right, all the way behind me and scanning the area like Dad told me to do when we were hunting deer, how you might have to wait to catch movement; he'd say, "Just scan slowly." So I was squatting down, kneeling, scanning, standing up, scanning and scanning. And still I hadn't seen anything. I was looking for a bear. The only thing I really noticed was this big tree that had got struck by lightning and stood out from all the other trees. It was down the embankment from the tracks, in a little dip. It was really wide, but I didn't focus on it because it wasn't a bear.

I didn't feel tingling like people say who have been zapped. I felt a very thick atmosphere. It felt like you were being pressed. The next voice that came into my mind was my foster dad's voice, and he said something that he commonly said: "Put one foot in front of the other before I plant mine knee-deep up your ass." I took off, and as I did this loud roar came up from the direction of that "tree." It sounded like an old bellowing drunk man yawning, and it dragged out. It hit me. It felt like it traveled *through* me. Tears flew out of my eyes. I pissed myself.

I ran to some people's yard, hit the ground, and rolled over to see what was about to attack me. There was nothing to see. And the people were on the porch. They were elderly people, and the man gets up and opens the screen door and says, "Get off my lawn! What are you doing? I don't know what you pissed off, but get off our lawn."

I'm horrified. My body is not catching up with me. I'm almost frozen. All pissed. All tears flowing down my face. And I'm pointing, and he was like, "I don't know what you pissed off, but don't bring him up here!" And I'm thinking, *Really? It sounds like Hell is behind me.*

So I pick myself up off the ground, and I'm having a hard time being able to move, and I drag myself off the lawn lengthwise because I want to make sure I'm on his lawn if something does run out of the brush and snatch me up.

13. Thom Powell: Oregon

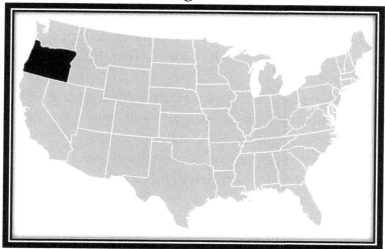

This testimonial appears in the documentary coda to Christopher Munch's film Letters from the Big Man. *This coda can be seen under the title "Sasquatch and Us" on the YouTube channel FirandCedar. Here, Powell clearly and succinctly expresses a common recognition: Sasquatch will interact with you only on their own terms. He is the author of several books, including* The Locals *and* Edges *of Science. I refer you also to his excellent blog, ThomSquatch.com.*

Once, I spent all night wood knocking, always whacking three times just like a good little BFRO Investigator, and finally gave up at the crack of dawn and drove home. And as soon as I got home, after traveling a hundred miles, I didn't even get out and shut the car door before "Whack Whack Whack!" came from the woods behind my house. The repercussions of that were obvious: Somebody was messing with *me*. I thought I was being the experimenter and the table just turned.

I found that the more I studied the subject, even in remote places, the more I got subtle indications that the subject was studying me. That really put a chill in me, because that's not something you can undo, how they—at least hypothetically—know where you live. So that was a sobering thought. But I also could see that there was no menace to it.

My initial reaction to it all was actually skepticism and doubt, because that's the science guy I still was. So it really took a lot before it all started to sink in.

So now when people say, "I've got them going on near me, what should I do?" the first thing I tell them is, "Well, you should decide what you want out of your 'research.' Do you want understanding or do you want proof? They're sort of mutually exclusive. If you chase after proof, you may or may not get it, but you're also going to find that it distances you from understanding and inspiration."

14. Elizabeth: Texas

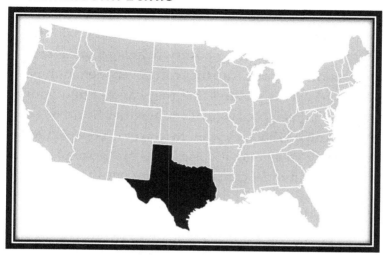

The varieties of mindspeak described here cover a broad spectrum from emotional impressions to indelible images to a generic voice that seems a translation of thought to the distinct voices of specific individuals. Also, note the very gradual escalation, spanning years, in the intensity of the interactions and the way that Elizabeth's patience and authenticity led eventually to a close and even playful relationship with one of the local females.

As far as I can tell, there are several forms of telepathic communication. One way that is pretty rare for me is a loud, clear, distinct voice that is obviously not internal monologue. I've heard a few that were so loud that I would look around to see who spoke, although I was alone every time it happened and didn't hear them with my ears. This seems only to happen to me if one badly wants my attention and it's usually only my name.

There is another way, the main one for me, that seems to be about translation. They all sound basically the same in the translated form, but they radiate emotions when they communicate and each one feels different. I always ask who I'm speaking with and after a while they get to be familiar by associating their name with the feeling that I get from them. They are extremely emotional and sometimes they can be almost overwhelming if one is sad, angry, afraid, or in pain. And they can be very demanding.

The third way is pictures that they can put into your mind. This happens occasionally when they want to be sure that I know what they want to convey. These pictures are extremely clear and it's like they are permanently stamped in my mind. I can still see every one that they've ever sent as clearly as if it had just happened.

But let me back up…

In retrospect, I know they've been around my whole life, but I didn't consciously know it until 2004.

We were sitting here one night, and I heard a bunch of coyotes just outside the back door. I went to the door and shined a flashlight out there but couldn't see them, so I went to the front door and shined the light out there and hit these two big eyes. They were kind of a pinkish red. They looked like two reflectors just shining back at me from out in the pasture. No body, just those two eyes, and in a little bit, they went out.

Other little things were happening too, like howls at night. We always left the windows up when it was warm enough, no shades. I had barely laid down in bed when I heard this loud howl, and the neighbors' cows started mooing. I ran to the window and listened. That howl was really something. It wasn't like a wolf. It wasn't really like anything I'd ever heard before.

Anyway, the cows all start stampeding to the north, and I ran through the house to the north window and listened, and the cows stopped when they got to the fence, and the howls kept on going. So it was a howl and then a bunch of mooing and then more howls that fade off until I can't hear them anymore.

Another early episode. My husband would feed our cows alfalfa and they would always come running from the barn. They would run *over* you to get at it. Well, one morning he goes down there and puts the hay down, and the cows are all staying at the barn. He got to looking around and the fence was torn down, but instead of it being torn down like the cows ran out, it was torn down from the *other* side, like something ran in, pushed the wire into the pasture. The cows wouldn't come away from the barn for about three days.

And then, the lid on his feed barrel started being off, and some of the feed gone, and we thought, *What the heck? A raccoon couldn't get that lid off.*

I used to sit out and listen for them to come every evening. There were about three houses that had dogs that would bark as they came closer. When they would get to the woods behind the house, they would start their different whistles, frog noises, knocks, etc. Occasionally, I would see green eye glow, almost always down low on the ground. One time one of them was on the roof of an outbuilding, peeping over the top. I watched for a few minutes, then I said, "I can see your eyes." When I said that, they immediately went out.

At night, they would bump the house, throw rocks on the roof, and they had a way of making the metal roof pop exactly above wherever I would be in the house.

So it was all adding up.

The night before Thanksgiving, 2006, I went out on the porch to get some wood and I heard what sounded like a bear growling real loud. And then another one was howling from another spot. Back and forth, one then the other, like they were apart but were keeping each other located. They came across the pasture to the front of the house and then stopped making noise when they got to our pond. After a while, they picked up again and their calls faded off into the distance.

The next morning, first thing, I got up and went down to our pond, and I found what looked like a fist print and some partial tracks in the mud.

Later that day, Thanksgiving, we went down to my sister-in-law's house. She lives about three miles south of us. When I told her about it, she said, "Well, I'll tell you what, I heard the very same thing."

I said, "What?!"

She said, "Yeah, I had been to Walmart, and I just came home. It was late, and I was unloading groceries out of the car, and I heard those noises coming from the north, and I heard them go by here. It was so scary that I made Jim come out and hold a gun while I unloaded the rest of the groceries."

After that, things really got going. Interacting with them became an obsession. I spent most of every night either at an open window or sitting outside talking to them and watching them move around among the shadows, making various wildlife noises.

Every time I would open the door to go out, there would immediately be a loud knock or one of their familiar noises to show that they were out there. Sometimes a little pebble would come flying from behind the bushes and land close by. It was very addictive to feel that important to them. What reason could they have to be that interested in an old country grandma?

It seems that when some people first meet them, they think they are the only ones this is happening to and they are content to have their little private exchanges. I was the same, but eventually there was a need to find others like myself, so I started hinting to friends and searching the Internet and soon turned up many more "Bigfoot people." We all had more or less the same story to share, and some of us became even closer than family.

There was this group of females that would come up at night and stay right here behind the house. They had kids with them. I'd hear them all out there, and there was one of them that would go, "Woo hoo." And we'd do that back and forth!

I'd stay up half the night, sometimes till three o'clock, sitting there at the window, listening to them out there, and every so often there'd be a bunch of males coming through, with big howls and everything. Then I'd hear their howls running off. I guess they came to check on the women and kids. In the grass, I'd find little circles maybe two and a half feet across, like the babies lay down there. Not like deer bedding at all.

When the mindspeak started was when this one female would come up every night, the one who called out, "Woo hoo." I'd go to the window upstairs, and when it was cold I kept the blanket pulled down over it, and I'd stick my head out and listen. Sometimes she'd say, "Woo hoo," and I'd answer, and they'd knock, and I'd knock.

One night, I went up there, and I had just started to pull the blanket back and she was *real close* when she said, "Woo hoo," and it scared me because she knew before I even pulled that blanket back that I was there. And I hadn't been making noise. I was barefoot and sneaking. It scared me and I ran back downstairs.

Well, that hurt her feelings. After that, I'd go to the window and I'd "Woo hoo," and she wouldn't answer. And that went on for two or three nights, you know. Finally — this was about two o'clock in the morning — I was lying there in bed. I knew she was out there. In my mind, I said, "Okay, I'm sorry, I'm sorry I was scared. I didn't mean to be." I said, "It wasn't your fault. But I'm not going to say anything else to you until you 'Woo hoo' at me again."

Nothing happened. The next night, she came and she knocked, and I didn't respond. She rustled around and tapped on the house and broke sticks, and I wouldn't say anything out loud. In my head, I said, "I told you, I'm not saying anything till you say, 'Woo hoo.'" And before I even finished that thought, I heard "Woo hoo."

That was how I *really* knew about mindspeak. It hits you in waves. And it went on from there.

At first, I saw a lot of pictures, like a female sitting by a creek in a little grassy place, and there were wild onions I guess, little white flowers, and she was pulling them up, throwing them down, pulling them up, throwing them down. That was the first actual picture I saw. It didn't startle me. It just seemed natural. Everything was natural. I never really disbelieved that they existed, and nothing that happened ever seemed all that strange.

What really got me started talking to them was No-Bite.* A mutual friend put us in touch, and we talked a lot about our experiences, and that's when I realized that others were having the same things happening. then she told me about this guy in Alabama, Thomas H., who was able to talk to them no matter the distance. He'd picked up on the name of one of her visitors, Nantaya, and told her just to think the name. When she did, Nantaya answered, "What?!", and they were off and running.

So No-Bite told me, "Call Thomas." I talked to him, and he told me some things about my locals, including names. But I still couldn't hear their voices. No-Bite could, but it took me longer. One day, I said, "Is anybody out there?" And I heard back, "Maggie." And I thought, *Nah, Bigfoots aren't named Maggie.* I'm sure that wasn't her real name. It took a few weeks and some removal of the mental blocks and protection I had erected over a lifetime to get the hang of it.

After that, I could hear her. People ask what it sounded like, but it wasn't really what it sounded like, it was more what it *felt* like. It was like a thought, just like when you think something, but you can tell that it's not a thought because it's something that you weren't thinking. I mean, it's hard to explain. You don't hear it in your voice, but it's so clear that you almost think you do, and then you look around and you realize it wasn't.

Sometimes at night, I'll hear, "Hey, Elizabeth." Sometimes it's in my husband's voice. Sometimes a woman's. All different voices.

A teenager asked me one night what I was doing. I told her I was lying in bed reading a book. After a discussion on the reasons for reading a book, she said, "I know you're in bed." I asked how she knew, and she said, "I can see you." We had a "cannot/can too" argument for a few minutes and finally I asked how she could see me. She said, "I'm in the tree, looking in the window."

Soon, I was mentally talking to some of them and they were answering in ways that could not be mistaken for my imagination. But they used words and phrases that I never used and some that I didn't even understand, but it was always in English. We were perplexed that they understood and spoke English and one day, my friend asked her Bigfoot friend how she'd learned it. She said, "I don't speak English. I thought you were speaking my language." We marvel that we can understand each other — our two sides. It isn't as loud or clear as the other way and sometimes we do get things confused. They can usually make themselves understood if they really want to, but mostly it's only when it's to their benefit.

I don't know how much truth there was in the things they told us, mostly because I always had the impression that they were laughing at us when they answered our questions. There are emotions that come through with the words, and many of their answers came with a glib feeling that gave me pause as to whether or not it was true. In spite of the questionable truth value of any given answer, though, much of it did prove to be accurate over time. We asked hundreds of questions and usually got answers.

There was one who wanted to know why we have water running out of the side of the house sometimes. I told her that we not only have it running out of the side of the house, but it also runs out of walls on the inside. She didn't believe it at first, but finally she wanted to know why. The deeper I got into explaining about washing clothes and dishes and taking baths and flushing toilets, the more inadequate and overburdened with "stuff" I felt. I could tell that she thought it was an awful waste of time and effort, not to mention water.

I've asked them about coming out and joining the world community. Apparently, they don't think much of the idea. The first one I asked wouldn't even answer the question and the second one was barely civil about it. He said, "We don't need our domain controlled by humans. It's already protected by us." He said they would have nothing to gain and everything to lose by "coming out." Then he sneered something about ridiculous questions. So…it probably won't be happening anytime soon.

15. LeeAnn: Ontario

Here is a very different type of communication — a resonance or, as LeeAnn calls it, "a deep knowing." She has found herself guided to many hundreds of elaborate stick and tree structures within protected and highly regulated city forests and, after feeling "called" to a certain barely accessible stretch of river, located excellent Sasquatch tracks in the mud (pictured below).

My berry-picking encounter happened seven years ago.

I was by myself in the woods, a large area of Crown Land, along an old lumber road that was overgrown from being used for harvesting timber several years before. I'd been going in there for a few years to pick berries, as they grew along the old road. A little aside...I was an outdoor educator for many years in my teens and twenties and I know to always make lots of noise when walking back into the forest by myself. I know how healthy the black bear population is around our cottage, and I would never want to have an unexpected encounter. I was right in the middle of a tall mulberry bush. It was like a thick wall of vines, and the berries were the size of my thumb knuckle. I'd slowly and carefully weaseled my way in there, avoiding the thorns as much as I could, so that I was fully in the bush.

I'd been picking in there for a couple minutes, and all of a sudden I heard a massive exhale, like a deep guttural *grrrruuuuuhhh!* It was so clear and broad and deep, and it's like it made the insides of my own body resonate. I have no words to explain how that felt. Massive deep vibration. The guttural exhale instantly shook me to my core. I looked, and I saw what I now know was a juvenile Sasquatch step out from the back of the bush and walk away into the healthy, old, mixed forest. The entire berry bush shook as it stepped away. I am not sure if it shook the branches on purpose, or whether it was just the result of the Sasquatch stepping out of the bush. I realized in that moment it had to have been in there with me the entire time I had been picking berries. I never saw or smelled or heard anything. And I know for certain I had been yelling and singing my entire way in along the path. I was a young mother at the time, and the last thing I wanted was to get into serious trouble with a bear while berry picking for homemade jam.

I saw it walk away, I heard it walk away, I saw the deeply dark outline of its head and shoulders and body....and in that moment I felt such overwhelming fear. It was the most intense fight-or-flight moment I've ever had.

> I ran out of that bush. I dropped my berries,
> tore my way out of the bushes and I ran all
> the way back to the car, over a kilometre. I
> never looked back the entire way.[1]

After that, it took a long time for me to go back in the woods, but the following summer, I started to feel the tug, like I was being led back out there. This is seventy kilometers north of the city, by our family cottage. I was very nervous to be there again. I started noticing tree bends and star formations — sticks and branches that had been placed up in trees, either in the crooks or weaved in and around other branches. Some of them were really small, some bigger. I also found little "nests," bundles of sticks on the ground. And I'd never seen anything like this on the Internet. I didn't have the language for it, but it was like my eyes and my brain started seeing things I'd never seen before. I was seeing repeated patterns and shapes and designs in this one particular area by our cottage. On this old road in the forest, I started seeing all these bends across it and trees laid across it, like they were saying, "Don't go any farther. This is our space." And I obeyed because it made me really nervous.

One day, I did something I'd never ordinarily do. I went out right after a rain, and I found two really good prints in the wet leaves — clear toe definitions, the whole bit. I thought, *This is real! Something pulled me out here to find these.*

On the flip side, I think I went somewhere I wasn't supposed to one time. This was the fall of 2014. I was studying a hemlock tree about four inches across that looked snapped three feet off the ground. All the trees around it are standing. It was a tight canopy, so it was mind-boggling how just this one was snapped like that. And here's another thing, the leafy end of the tree was lying on the ground, but the snapped end was on top of the remaining base — just balanced up there not connected.

So I was standing there thinking, *Hmmm*. I was alone, broad daylight, and out of nowhere I get hit with the biggest dizzying sensation that made me feel completely off balance. My eyes rolled into the back of my head or just around and around, like when you have bed spins and you can't keep your eyes straight. My knees weakened instantly. I could barely stand. Adrenaline rushed through my arms, my legs, my gut. Also, my hearing went all wonky. The sound of the forest increased like the volume knob was just turned way up, and everything became distorted. So not just the volume but also the bass, treble. Everything became this massive, indistinguishable noise. And to top it off, I was experiencing this huge panic infiltrating my body head to toe.

I knew I had to run, but it was really difficult because I was so off balance. I was only twenty feet from the path, but I couldn't even *try* to run over there. Once I'd stumbled back to the path and started back towards the road, every step I took it left me and left me, and my eyes stopped rolling around. My ears started working normally again. I still had the adrenaline running through my veins for maybe an hour.

Well, that put me off the trail for quite a while. It took a lot of courage to go back there in the spring. I changed my approach. I started doing a lot of audio recording instead of exploring, and for some reason that's when I began finding much better structures back down south, within the city limits where I live with my family most of the time. We have an extensive system of ravines and river bottoms running through protected park land forests. It's against the law to camp here, start a fire, or disturb any of the vegetation, including trees. And yet, I kept finding these formations. That's when things really opened up and my intuition became honed in to where these are.

So yeah, it was strange. It was like the lines of communication were opening up on both levels. The more I did audio recording up at the cabin and they willingly let me hear them, the more I was finding — being allowed or *led* to find — down in the city forests. On audio, I'd get wood knocks, bipedal footsteps, pebbles thrown at the sides of the toolshed, and this very cool drumming; the dock was pulled up out of the lake so the plastic floats underneath were exposed, and you can hear someone going boom boom boom BOOM...boom BOOM boom boom, and that's the only surface nearby that they could have been using to make this hollow sound.

Every year, I've kept doing audio at the cabin — never trying to hide cameras — and the results have only increased in volume of activity, nearness, and clarity. It's like the trust is continuing to develop. The footsteps are more pronounced now; I've got little footsteps, definitely bipedal, running by the microphones. Things have just continued to progress.

Meanwhile, I've discovered hundreds and hundreds of structures down south, probably seven or eight hundred — no exaggeration. [You can see a great many of these, and hear audio clips, on her YouTube channel, "Southern Ontario Sasquatch."]

In the beginning, I was like, *Seriously? Here?* I couldn't believe I was finding these complicated structures in these city forests so close to civilization. I just kept finding more and more and more. I kept reserving judgment and thinking, *Okay, probably human.* And then two showed up over a really short period of time in an area that I'd been walking past a lot. That was the clincher for me because this is way off trail, quite wet and muddy on the way in there.

What a paradigm shift. Coming to that awareness of possibility was so exciting and mind blowing that I was totally hooked, lined, and sinkered.

And so I took it upon myself to explore one particular river. I'd never been farther than this one pocket. I started researching that river system, finding ways in, learning the trails, and taking the time to also get *off* the trails, going along game trails, following subtle signs. The farther I went, the more structures I found. The passion was strong, and I was exceptionally motivated. I felt the pull more and more.

That's when I started waking up in the middle of the night. I would find myself visualizing the river, surveying its system in my mind's eye. I *knew* I had to check out this place or that place next, go this way or that way, eyeball some creek that drains into the river valley. *How does it all fit together? I've got to figure it out.*

Now, I'd never been on foot to these spots. I started getting up early on weekends, while my family was still sleeping, on ridiculously colds days or wet days. There were days I was so tired, but *I gotta go!* The curiosity was just getting the best of me. And I'm not kidding, *every* time I went out to a spot for the first time — *boom.* And the more I found, the more I was waking up in the night because I would remember seeing a waterway in passing that I didn't even know the name of, but I knew I had to get back there. *Soon.*

After going down this one river and finding dozens and dozens and dozens of structures, I also started noticing some were changing and being rebuilt and modified, new ones popping up over a very short period of time. And never any people around.

I learned that this river joined another river, so then I followed *that* river — and found the exact same things. I'm like, *Holy moly! They're using the rivers… Is it for travel, is it to cover up their tracks, is it some connection with the water and the energies of the water? What's going on here?*

And then, I branched out into other rivers and ravines. I had no idea how many small creeks drain into these rivers, and I've scrambled up so many of these *tiny* draws and found structures…*way* off trail.

I would piece my journeys together. There was only so much ground I could cover at one time before I had to go back home and be Mom and take care of my family and do the things I had to do for work.

I started being directed even during the day. I remember one time at work, I was sitting at my desk, my brain in a million different directions, and all of a sudden, *ka-boom*, I had the message planted in my head: *You need to go here. This is where you need to go next.* I could feel it. It was a physical sensation, like butterflies. It came with the name of the river, but I'd never been there. I looked it up on Google Maps.

This happened many times, where the message was planted during the day, and I'd go out. Not to downplay the sacredness of the experience, but it became almost comical. I'd check out this new area, and…*jackpot!* I couldn't explain it, still can't. It was a deep knowing combined with an emotional excitement...those butterflies each time...like I couldn't *wait*.

One time, I ran into this World War II vet, quite elderly, and he had spent most of his life since the war visiting this one beautiful park where I met him. There was this huge wetland and tons of protected flora and fauna, and he was like the guardian. He was the only person granted permission to walk off trail because he knew where the bobolinks nested. He knew where the deer hung out. His feet would be the last feet to step on anything that shouldn't be stepped on. He walked so softly and with such reverence. From time to time, he would take school children to really special, designated locations to teach them, but otherwise, it was strictly off limits.

I asked him, "So what's with all these stick and tree formations?" He looked at me, and he gave me this grin. He had this twinkle in his eye and said, "There are some things we may never fully understand." He was looking at me as if he knew, but he didn't want to shock *me*.

Here's something else that blew me away. Where I work is situated on an old-growth forest ravine. It actually connects with the river where I first found structures years ago. Behind my main building, there's a path to another building where I exercise, and down below is this beautiful forest, and it's a part you can't really even walk to because it's too steep, and there's some dumped material left over from construction. It's just not a place you'd go. But every time I'd walk by it, I'd look down there and think, *That would be a perfect spot for a structure. Wouldn't that be amazing if one showed up right there?* I'd been thinking this for a couple years.

So this past August, I went back there, and I looked over the railing, and *boom*, there was a fresh, free-standing structure that hadn't been there a month earlier. I scrambled down, and it was about five feet tall and incorporated maybe twenty different sticks — beautifully balanced and new, exactly where I'd been imagining it.

Last spring, 2018, I was poking along a river I'd been working for three years. There was this one section of it I could not for the life of me figure out how to get down to.

Too many bends from the north, and the water was too deep to cross. On the south side, there was this big wetland, and the trails just ended, leaving this whole middle section inaccessible. Finally, somehow, I got an idea for where to look. I went on Google Maps and found a little opening off of a road that I didn't know was even there.

It was a really tight scramble down a long, steep V, lots of fallen trees to climb over. But once I got down there, I came onto a wider trail that looked old, disconnected from all the trails I knew. And then, I found the prints on the riverbank. I totally didn't expect this. I was just looking for structures.

During the previous week, we'd had a major snowstorm and then a quick melt so that all the rivers were swollen. You could hear on the radio, "Stay away from the rivers. Stay away from the rivers." There was so much water just pounding through those valleys.

The day I got there, it looked like the water had just barely receded because even though it was well below zero (Celsius), the sand and mud hadn't had time to freeze yet.

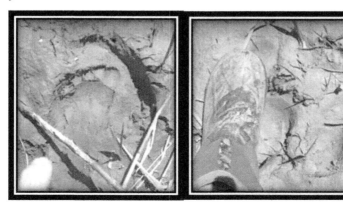

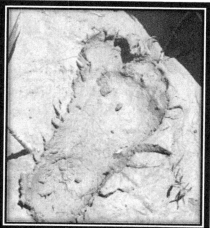

You can see this discovery unfold in real time on LeeAnn's video "Footprints along a River." If you're new to her YouTube channel, Southern Ontario Sasquatch, I'd also recommend the following videos to start with: "Who Are You?", "Stunning Changes Over the Last Week!", "Storytelling in a Magical Forest," "Dream-Inspired Discoveries," "Massive Arched Bird Nest Structure," "Creativity of the Sasquatch," "Strange Vocals," and "An Evening of Wood Knocks."

They've steered me wrong just a couple of times, not many. It's made me wonder, *Am I off? Am I pushing the subject instead of just being receptive and gravitating at the right time?* I think I'm at the point right now where I love these creations and these areas so much, it's like visiting dear old friends, so I almost can't go wrong. Sometimes, if I've had a rough day at work, I'll drive a half hour extra on the way home just to visit one. They ground me and bring me back to all the enthusiasm and awe over the past few years. They act as guideposts for me, reminding me of parts of myself, where I've come from. A lot of my visits now are about deepening the connection and continuing to honor them.

And audio. I'm in love with audio. When I'm putting out the recorder at night, that's a very personal and sacred moment. Very private. It's similar to being in a church. My heart feels like it's just cracking right open, and then I find myself saying things I wouldn't ordinarily say. I don't even know if they're true, like I'll call them Guardians of the Forest, the Ancient Ones, Ancient Brother and Sisters, the Keepers of the Energy of the Woods. In those moments, when I'm in the dark, in the woods, by myself, reaching out, I get teary, goosebumps, a tremendous amount of emotion just surging through me...not images but deep feelings of *This is who I'm communing with*.

16. SnowWhiteBigfoot: Ohio

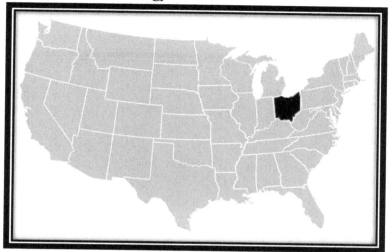

As you will have noticed, a common thread running through many of the foregoing testimonials is Sasquatch's reaching out to children through various forms of mindspeak. Here, we have an apparent case of the same unfolding in real time on video.

The researcher who goes by SnowWhiteBigfoot has carefully chronicled, in her YouTube series "My Bigfoot Diary," a years-long experiment in communicating with her local Sasquatch group through objects given, received, relocated, and rearranged. I discuss her work on pages 159-172 of *Next of Kin Next Door*. I also interview her on YouTube: "The Nearness of You Podcast: Episode #2."

The video at issue in terms of mindspeak is called "Was Annabelle Talking to Her Bigfoot Friend Again?" on the SnowWhiteBigfoot YouTube channel. We see that her three-year-old granddaughter Annabelle is drawn to a tall, dense area of pampas grass at the edge of the yard, waves, and says, "Hello," although there is apparently nothing there. At the 6:32 mark, you can even see her hesitate for a moment, exactly as if she's heard her name being called — as in so many of the memories shared here in Part 2.

But how could a Sasquatch be hiding in there in broad daylight, especially with adults around? Perhaps it wasn't. Perhaps the girl heard her name and looked to the only place that seemed like a hiding spot. Maybe the message was "I'm here in the grass." (They like to play with us.) Perhaps the "speaker" was two hundred yards away in the forest.

I realize that this incident amounts to no more than circumstantial evidence. The grandmother does not wish to interview Annabelle directly about what she is experiencing because she doesn't want to "lead the witness"; she's waiting for the girl to volunteer such information.

The plot thickens, however, in the next video, "My Bigfoot Diary 62," when SnowWhiteBigfoot finds a new object on the front porch railing, a plastic 0, placed directly over the head of the figure meant to represent Annabelle.

Meanwhile, on the front porch, the stuffed monkey figure is moved, overnight, so that it appears to be peeking out from behind the lantern — quite like someone hiding in, say, a clump of pampas grass.

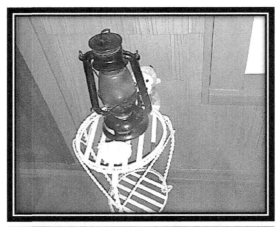

17. Robin: Michigan, South Carolina, Texas

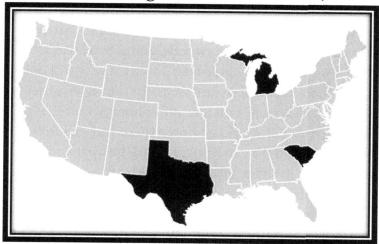

This final testimonial has it all — early childhood dialogue that nobody believed, intense emotional contact, all forms of mindspeak unfolding across the years, instructive and cautionary episodes showing the importance of trust and the maintaining of strict boundaries and "safe zones," a hilarious prank played on a cable guy, a loving and mutually protective relationship with several Sasquatch, like members of the family, in Michigan and South Carolina, and then, on the flip side, a terrifying standoff with a cold-hearted alpha male in Texas.

I don't remember a time when I *wasn't* telling people about Bigfoot and stick structures and everything else. Nobody would believe what I said because I was born in 1964 when Bigfoot was not a topic that anyone knew about. My mom said that when I was two and three, I would talk to her, and she assumed it was all about a child's imaginary friend. She said I would talk about this big hairy person that was way, way bigger than Dad—

who was six four — and had all this hair all over his body and his face, yet around his head it was longer, "like the mane of a lion. "

Back then, it was okay to let your kid ride their bike down to the corner. We lived in a subdivision, but our subdivision was right next to woods, and when I was four and five, I would ride my little bike down to the end of our road, and there were these dirt mounds from where they would dump dirt from building other homes, and you'd ride up and down. I would go down there and sit next to the woods, and I'd play in the sand and the dirt, and the Foots would be in there, and they would talk to me in my head. Then, I'd go home and they'd still talk to me. I could carry on complete conversations with them. It was my normal. I didn't know any different.

As I got older, I got tired of asking other people, "What, you can't *hear* this?" So I just kept it to myself. At first, when I was a teenager, I thought I was nuts. But then I thought, *Why am I not nuts in any other part of my life? If I'm crazy, I should have crazy tendencies in other areas.* But really, I've never worried too much. Maybe it was a calming sense that I got from them, but I've never been like *Oh my God, what was that?* I never had that moment. It was just... me and them.

People automatically believe that with telepathy, you're going to hear this voice in your head. But if you wait for that voice, good luck with it, because you may never know that you're communicating. It comes in several forms. It can be a random thought that you don't know why you're having. They'll make you think that that thought is yours. They can show you pictures that look like you're watching a movie. And a lot of people don't realize that it can also be a feeling. The Foots know how to project their feelings on you — good, bad, ugly.

One time, I'm out there walking in the woods, and all of a sudden, I felt this intense, intense fear. When they project an emotion on me, I get this clear sense of what it's about. I automatically get the whole story behind it. In that case, I understood that there was a female out there with a child, and she was concerned. You see, I had had company over that day, and I had told this person, "I do *not* want you out back in the woods unless you're with me. It's not for your safety. It's for *their* comfort. You're in their home, I just pay the taxes on it."

He didn't listen. And so when I went out to do my normal walk-about, he'd snuck out back, and that's what she was feeling, this intense fear because here was this stranger in a sensitive area.

We had this low part where the water would pool, and there was a bunch of reeds, and they would take the kids and babies down there, and if they wanted to go hunt they'd put the babies in with the reeds where they'd be nice and safe. Nobody was going to go in there because it was so wet. So she had put one of the kids down in there — only about five or six months old — and as she went to leave it, this fool (my company) starts walking through.

She saw him, and she was terrified, and that's what I got. It literally felt like somebody just sucker-punched me in the gut. I felt every ounce of her fear, and at the same time, I got the whole situation projected. It's almost like you're in there living it with them.

This whole thing starts mental, but it becomes physical. Once you connect with them, with a core group that you're very in tune with, it does become a physical thing. You're going to feel their emotions. There are times when it's a normal voice and it's not that loud, and then I get ones that are in a panic because something bad's going on, and it's literally yelling, like somebody's got this megaphone in your head, screaming.

When there's a bunch of them excited and all talking at once, I don't have any ill effects other than I'll get dizzy. It feels like the whole room is spinning. I had to learn that when they get like that, I have to acclimate myself and separate the individuals. I tell them, "One at a time," and depending on the group, they'll listen or not.

Back in the early 1990s, still in Michigan, the Foots would steal my chicken eggs and get into things around the yard or barns. At that time, they would project feelings more than anything. I had seen a few running through the yards at night when they thought everyone was asleep.

One night at about 11:30, out of the blue I got the strongest desire to go out in the woods. Now the woods I wanted to go to was across the street. You then walked through a forty-acre area of plowed farmland before reaching the trees.

It was this intense feeling like I had no control. I had small children at the time, so I called my friend around the corner and asked her daughter to come babysit. She came over immediately and brought her older sister, who wanted to come with me. Also, another friend I had told I was going out refused to let me go alone in the dark. The area had coyotes, cougars, etc.

So the three of us set out into the dark. I took no flashlights and for some reason I was adamant that we could not use them. My friends thought I was nuts. So we go out there. I seemed to know exactly where I was going, yet I had never been there before. I walked through and then behind the forty acres. Then I made a sharp turn into the woods. I had déjà vu. I was making all kinds of turns and stops like I knew where I was going. I eventually got way ahead of my friends. I could hear them calling in the distance, yet I ignored them and kept going like I was in a rush. I walked through the most dense woods I have ever been into in my life. Yet I kept going.

Eventually, the woods were so deep I couldn't walk through it. The only option was a narrow deer run. My friends kept calling. Once inside the deer run, I had to walk hunched over because it was so tight in there. I remember thinking that if a deer were to run through there I would be trampled. I couldn't get out of the run because the brush was too thick. It was completely dark except for a full moon. I kept going until I thought I heard someone talking to me.

It was mindspeak. They said you showed us your home, now you may see ours. It felt like whatever mind control that had been used now stopped. I was fully aware I was there and what had happened. I asked, "What am I doing here?" I was told I was safe. I looked just ahead and to the left. I was stunned to say the least. There was this huge nest. It reminded me of the sugared Easter eggs I had as a child where you looked inside and saw three-dimensional pictures in them.

This nest was approximately four feet off the ground. Underneath was all brush, sticks, leaves, dirt. The sides were woven around in an upward pattern. It had a top to it. The whole thing was enclosed except for a large opening in the front. It was very tall, much taller than I am. The opening was large enough for even a huge Foot to crawl in. In fact, this whole nest could certainly hold more than a few of them. The top was tightly woven. It definitely looked water tight. The sides were super-thick too. I have never seen anything like this in my life and haven't seen anything like it since.

There was no odor at all. It all smelled just like the trees and leaves. The opening was inside the deer run. You could only access if you were inside that corridor. They would have to have gone through it on all fours.

I could still hear my friends yelling way in the background. They had no idea where I'd gone. I opened my mouth to call to them, but before I could speak I was told not to—that they wouldn't be safe. I turned around back towards where I came from and saw three Foots standing there. One male, one female, and a small child. The child appeared to be a girl. They stood there staring at me. I felt nothing but love coming from them. They never tried to hurt me or scare me in any way. I think they may have done something to calm me. The male was black, the female was a brownish color, and the little girl was brown and slightly reddish. I just stood there stunned. I looked at them and the nest. I felt that they were going to tell me something.

Before they could, my friends got too close. Although they were not in the deer run they were out by the opening. The female told me I must go and that nobody could know about this place. I would see them again, she said. I would go home and be safe. Nothing would hurt me on the way back. Then she said not to let my friends know, as they were not ready. I turned and walked out of the deer run.

Again, I was completely calm. I rejoined my friends and never told them what I'd seen. It was so dark and the brush so dense they never saw the opening I emerged from. We calmly walked back to the house. My friends were worried we were lost. Yet again, I zig-zagged though the fields and wooded area and took us right back home.

Of course, I wanted to find it again later but had no idea how to. I remembered going, but parts of how I got there are missing from my memory. I remember being with my friends and them calling me. I ignored them but it's a total blank where I was.

In the fall was bow hunting season. There had to be a lot of hunters out, and everywhere that they found arrows, the Foots would collect them and set them on my porch. I would get thirty, forty, fifty arrows every fall. My sons used to bow hunt too. Never got a deer, but they had an awful lot of fun trying every year. They'd go into the back yard for target practice.

This one time, the boys wanted to practice with the bow and arrow, and I told them *not* to shoot arrows into the Foots' woods. The rule was the Foots can take the woods in the front, and you can hunt in the back. I'd let the clan know, so they'd all go to the front where everybody'd be safe. This generally worked out well.

So this one day, I told the boys, "You can go *parallel* with the woods, but you may not shoot into the woods because they're going to feel threatened. They have children out there."

I'm in the house, and I hear the boys laughing. Then I hear in my mind, "We're going to teach them a lesson."

A few minutes later, my son comes in. "Mom, you better talk to your Bigfoots. Look, they tried to hit me with this *log*." And he's holding this log in his hand.

I said, "They would never hit you with that on purpose. What did you do?"

He said, "I just bent over to pick up my arrow?"

"You mean the arrow that wasn't supposed to make it into the woods?"

"I'll show you where they threw it at me."

Well, it was *just* inside the Foots' woods. I said, "You guys were screwing around out here and laughing." They had accidentally shot it sideways into that woods. This was a nice-sized chunk of wood they threw at him!

Boundaries are always extremely important to the Foots.

After we moved into our house here in South Carolina last year, the cable guy came out. We're in the woods here too, and once you've been connected to the Foots, they can locate you wherever you go if it's forest. So the cable guy is messing around outside, and it's getting dark. He goes, "Ma'am, I'll just come back tomorrow," and I'm like, "No, we're not playing this game. I need to get on the Internet."

I knew there were Foots out there, because as soon as they come near I can feel the energy change, and my head feels different. My head feels like there's something filtering through it, trying to pick through it. I said to them, "Who's out there?" And it got quiet. I said, "I'm not going to hurt you. I just want to know that you're out there." Then, I heard, "We are here."

So pretty soon, this cable guy comes in the house again, and he's white as a ghost. Before he even came in the door, I heard laughter in my head, and I'm like, "What have you done now?" Because they are serious pranksters. They love it. They have a wicked sense of humor.

He said, "Ma'am, I'm sorry, but I'm from New Jersey."

I said, "Okay?"

"I'm not used to this woods, but there's stuff out in your woods. That strip of trees that goes next to your property?"

I said, "Yeah?" I already know what he's going to say.

"I don't know what it is, but whatever's in that bunch of bush is *huge*." He said, "It's huge. I didn't really see it other than I saw shadows, but there's branches snapping in a really big area, so whatever's in there's gotta take up space."

I said, "Oh, it's fine. Go finish the installation."

He's like, "No. I don't even want to go back out to the truck."

In my head, they're cracking up. And I'm like, "When this guy's gone, you all are in so much trouble." They're projecting the emotions of laughing onto me, so I'm trying not to laugh.

I told the guy, "Listen, I don't want you to do anything you're not comfortable with. Just leave the stuff and come back."

He said, "Well, yeah, I still need to get more wire for the hook-up anyway."

The next morning, my husband gets up to go to work. When he opens the door, here is this wad of *wires*. I don't know where they got it. I don't even know what it was for originally. It wasn't anything we could use, but all they knew was the guy needed wires. This huge pile of wires lay on the front porch, up against the door.

A new cable guy arrives and tells us, "Yeah, I don't know what went down here last night, but that guy would not come back."

I say, "I don't know what the issue was. Must have been a raccoon or something in the brush over there." And all I can hear is laughter.

Later, here in South Carolina, I went to leave my house one morning, and as I'm pulling out of the driveway, I hear this panicked voice, "You've got to help me, you've got to help me! They're coming, they're coming!"

I said, "Okay, first of all, calm down. Where are you?"

"I'm not far from you, but the men are here, and they've got a gun."

I'm like, "Show me a picture." I turned out of my driveway, and he's showing me pictures of trees, and of course I'm in the woods so I ask if he can be a little more specific. I just got bombarded with every form of telepathy at once. I'm in a panic.

Less than a half mile away, here are these three men outside of their pick-up truck, and they're standing on the edge of the swamp, and they're pointing to the back of the swamp, and they're making whoop calls. Unless you know what a Foot is, you're not making that call. And yes, one of them did have a gun leaning up against the truck.

My first instinct was to stop and go totally postal, but then I thought, *No, because if they know I know what's in these woods, they're never going to leave the area, and it'll no longer be a safe zone.*

So I told the freaked-out Foot, "You need to go back into my back property because that's a safe zone. That's why everybody hangs here."

He said, "I'm trying to get back there."

"You need to find a way."

He did, and then he hung around here for about three days before he was finally brave enough to meander off.

He was a new one. See, my core guys are here, and then we've got a couple different clans that come through here.

I have this row of shrubs and scrub trees that go along either side of my property, and it makes a great privacy fence. I went out there one day and this one portion was flat, like you could've driven a bus through it, and I'm like, "All right, I don't know who's pushing everything down, but this is my privacy fence. What the hell?"

So I go out there the next morning, and it looks like somebody has been in there trying to pull all these branches and stuff up, you know, trying to stand it up again. And then about ten feet beyond it is a little spot that was nice and full before, and now all the branches are broken off. It looks like they've all been making room and sitting in there, trying to fix the fence.

My son was working on this jeep he had bought. He was about sixteen at the time, and he and his friend and my two older kids wanted to test-drive this jeep. I said, "Okay, just go a couple miles down the dirt road, then get back here. I don't want you off joyriding."

So off they went. It should have been a five-minute trip and it's now been twenty minutes. So Redd pipes up — the Foot I talk to most — and gives me this overwhelming sense of love. And he says, "It's going to be okay. They're all right, nobody's hurt."

"What do you mean nobody's hurt?" I'm panicked.

And he's like, "Calm down. Just know that they're all okay."

"Where are my children?"

"There's been an accident. I'm watching them now. Help is coming."

Just then, this police car pulls into the driveway, and I can see my two older kids in the back seat. The officer gets out and says, "There was an accident. Your son is back there waiting for someone to come pick up the vehicle."

I was just in shock, but the whole time the cop's talking to me, Redd's in the background, and it feels like I'm getting a physical hug from him—just pure love.

What had happened was they went around a corner and something broke underneath the vehicle. It rolled. They had some concussions and contusions, but they were fortunate because I saw the vehicle later, and they could have died. They all had seatbelts on.

See, people don't think this stuff is real, but it's as real as it gets. Some Foots are loving, and some are the complete opposite.

I took a trip out to Texas to see my friend Elizabeth [whom we met earlier in Part 2] and to help a man set up a habituation site. When I met him at the spot, I said, "I'm telling you right now, this is not what I'd consider a safe area. You have some here that are nice, but you also have a lot more that are not, and they don't want you here." It was a hundred-acre plot that backed up to a nature preserve, and I could tell they took it as *their land*. Nobody lived on it, but he happened to know the people that owned the hundred acres, and they had consented for him to use it as a research area.

There were three older homes on it that were abandoned, and it looked like these people literally left in the middle of the night because everything they owned was still there. I mean *everything*. And the houses looked like somebody had bashed in the windows, kicked in the doors. There were animal bones on the front porches.

We drove around in his truck and stopped at this kind of alcove in the forest. When we got out, I noticed a deer feeder unit. Hunters fill them up with corn. These things aren't cheap, and this was a huge one, and they'd just left it behind. As I look on the ground, I'm seeing deer bones everywhere. And cattle bones, though there were no cattle around here, so they must've dragged them over here.

I looked at this guy. "You just showed up at their dining room table. What do you think you're doing here?" He had his grandchildren with him, and these kids are now out of the truck and they're running all over the place. Two girls and a boy. And there's a tree stand here too, this old abandoned tree stand with nailed boards for a ladder. As they start up the ladder, you could hear the Foots coming in from all different sides. I could hear them with my ears and in my mind, both.

The kids heard it too. They said, "We can hear branches breaking."

And in my mind, the alpha male is going, "Get out. You have no business here. Get out."

So I go to my friend, "You need to get these kids out of here now, this is dangerous. This is a serious, *serious* situation."

And he's like, "Oh no, Robin, Honey, it's fine."

And I'm like, "Don't you *Honey* me, you jackass." I was furious, and I was getting the alpha male's rage hitting me too. So I walked up to the base of the tree stand. He was at the backside of this alcove in the woods, and there were other Foots all around the sides. I was determined to hold my ground, and this male is screaming loud in my head, "You will leave now."

I say, "I will not leave." The kids can't figure out what's going on. They're still up on the hunting platform. They don't want to come down because they don't know what's going on. In my mind, I say again, "I'm not leaving without the kids."

He says, "You *will* leave without the kids." I hate to say it, but they do take children.

"No," I answered, "I will *not*."

My clueless friend is standing there behind me and just watching all of this unfold. He doesn't know what to think or do, but he knows because of the position I was standing in that I'm talking to somebody.

I think the alpha male is surprised that I'm dumb enough to stand up to him.

I say to the kids, "I want you guys to come down and go back over by Grandpa."

And they're like, "Well, we want to see the Bigfoot." I'm thinking, *You're going to see it more than you want.*

"C'mon down and I'll take everybody for ice cream!" I walk past the kids so that I'm between them and him. I knew exactly where the alpha was standing because I could see his outline in the shade. I couldn't really see him because he was partially cloaked.*

I said, "Here's the thing, I will leave. I don't want to be here. I'm not here to disrespect you in any way, but I will not leave without these children." I said, "They didn't know they weren't allowed to be here." I apologized to him completely because they're not going to let you get the upper hand. "I'm sorry that we're here. They did not *know*. I will take the children and we will leave."

He said, "You will leave the children."

"I will *not* leave the children."

Now the kids started down, and I backed up so I was level with them again. I wasn't about to turn my back. I was standing next to a palmetto bush that came up past my waist.

That's when he bluff-charged me. You couldn't see him, but you could feel the ground vibrate, and I could hear him screaming in my head. My friend didn't hear the screams, the kids didn't hear the screams, but they could all feel the pounding footsteps.

I was afraid to move. The kids were almost at ground level now. He came so close before he stopped that he completely leveled the palmetto bush and blew the hair

---

*Okay, here we go—cloaking. I've hesitated to broach this topic because the concept is, for most, even more difficult to accept than telepathy. Let me do my best to explain what I think is taking place.

In my 2016 eBook *Electric Sasquatch: How a Natural Force May Explain "Supernatural" Powers*, I discuss a range of behaviors and phenomena associated with Sasquatch that are, it seems to me, clearly electromagnetic in nature.

back off my shoulders. It was the craziest, craziest thing. The tree stand is maybe twenty-five feet from the bush, and the kids saw the bush get destroyed — the palm fronds going everywhere — and my hair fly back, and they started right back up the damn ladder.

I still held my ground. How I did it I don't even know. The kids are climbing, and I go, "Hey, you guys, they're just playing. Look at the stick on the ground ha ha ha, they threw the stick at the bush!" Anything I could think of. "They're being so silly, they're just showing off."

I'm laughing, I'm giggling, I'm lying out my ass to these kids, and they said, "Oh, we thought they were being mean."

"Oh, no, they love you, they think you're adorable."

"Oh, okay."

So the kids finally come back down, and my friend is like, "Robin!"

---

*For example, thousands of people have reported the experience of being "zapped" in the presence of this species; the hairs on their arms and the back of their necks stand on end;
they feel disoriented, dizzy, or nauseated; sometimes they are briefly paralyzed, locked in place for seconds or minutes.

The go-to explanation for these symptoms has long been infrasound, which can certainly cause them in its targets and is a well-known capacity in large mammals such as whales, elephants, and the big cats. But infrasound cannot disrupt electronic equipment, and this is a second commonly reported experience out in the field — fully charged batteries suddenly drained; cameras freezing or dying; walkie-talkies reduced to static.

I could quote examples all day of this so-called "Bigfoot curse," but here are just two.

I tell him, "Start. The. Truck." I say to the kids, "Go get in the truck. I'm going to stay and say goodbye to our friends first."

"You *are*? We want to say goodbye too."

I made them run back to the truck, and their grandfather is like, "Robin, come on!"

I said, "Start the truck and open my door." I didn't budge till those kids were safely inside. I backed up all the way. As we pulled away another one came running and banged the back side panel of the truck, I mean *hard*.

---

*   **A researcher quoted in Nick Redfern's *The Bigfoot Book*:**
Although we had tested all of our electronic equipment the night before, had charged up batteries where necessary, and had even put new batteries in all of our equipment that needed them, practically without exception all of our new equipment failed. The laptop battery… lasted just three minutes before failing. The batteries in our tape recorders also failed.

David Ellis of The Olympic Project:
I was walking in the woods at a habituation site and felt a pain high on my leg. I reached into my pocket and pulled out a 9-volt battery that had suddenly become so hot I couldn't even hold it.

This potent effect is not limited to equipment, however. Countless researchers and at-home witnesses have experienced the same telltale impact on their bodies.

Denise in Maine (Part 2):
[After my encounter in the yard,] I stood in the mudroom, and my whole body had…like…*electricity* in it, and I couldn't stop shaking. And I started crying, and my son started crying. He goes, "What's going on with you?" I

go, "I don't know! I can't stop shaking, I can't stop shaking. "

Rita, quoted in my book *Our Life with Bigfoot: Knowing Our Next of Kin at Habituation Sites*:
One of the more profound experiences I had that afternoon was getting "zapped." All of a sudden, I felt nervous. I felt a little nauseated, and my head was bothering me. I felt very unwelcome.

And something else, too. It's like when you're about to put your hand on a TV screen and you get that tingling all over the surface of your hand. It was like that all over my whole body, and worse on my arms and legs.

Stewart in Oklahoma (Part 2):
It was a similar feeling to being surrounded by a high-tension, static electrical field, which makes your hair stand up on end. A very pronounced feeling.…. I asked my host if I could use my night vision scope to possibly view them. She said yes, and I turned on the scope, but it wouldn't work. I recycled the switch and it still didn't work. I was freaking out at this turn of events because it was a brand new item and I'd had no trouble with it the two previous nights.

In my book *Next of Kin Next Door*, I quote researchers Mark Zaskey and Marc Abell reporting, respectively, that "My camera started acting up, and I felt like I had some type of electricity flowing through me. I got nauseas and panicked like I'd never felt before," and that "I felt energy surging through my body" when his camera suddenly froze. See the YouTube video "Episode of Sasquatch Electricity 2."

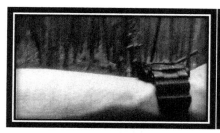

Shortly before the encounter, the hairs on Marc's arms stood up even though, as he says on the video, "I'm not scared."

With an eye toward a unified understanding of the empirical evidence, then, I've proposed that Sasquatch employs an electromagnetic field (EMF) to accomplish the above two aims — disabling our gear and zapping us — as well as distorting light/vision (see below).

Nor are versions of this same capacity particularly rare in nature. Many marine creatures, birds, and insects make use of EMFs for perception (*electroreception*), communication, and defense, and there is even one primate species, closely related to Sasquatch, that occasionally activates a similar potential — *Homo sapiens.*

Certain individuals are called "electric people" and have been shown to emit electromagnetic energy that disables watches and cell phones, causes light bulbs to explode, etc. Though currently unexplained, this strange propensity has been well documented, as in Chapter 1 of *The Electric Shock Book* by Michael Shallis, in Hilary Evans' *Sliders: The Enigma of Streetlight Interference*, and in numerous online sources such as ThoughtCo.com, May 15, 2017.** It seems clear to me that our zoological next of kin has evolved a far more prodigious and yet more manageable form of that which annoys and curses electric people and those who come in contact with them.

**Some people report that electronic machines shut off or go haywire in their presence. "One time, I had to have my neck lasered in a series of appointments," says Sarah, "and the machine broke six times — on six different occasions." Battery-operated watches are frequent victims of these people, and the

*   I'll also mention here that many field researchers and residents at habituation sites report seeing flashing lights in the forest and/or "orbs" that float along aimlessly or, occasionally, proceed in an apparently controlled fashion, as though being consciously directed — an observation so bizarre that it was long dismissed as an unrelated quirk of nature or mere hallucination before the sheer number of such reports, in association with Sasquatch activity, forced investigators to begin taking them seriously. My own supposition is that these phenomena are further manifestations of Sasquatch's electromagnetic capacity, perhaps akin to the phenomenon of ball lightning.

Ball lightning, depicted in this 1886 drawing by G. Hartwig, puzzled Aristotle 2300 yeas ago and Nicola Tesla in 1904.

** trait might run in families. "I have the problem with watches and appliances," Murph says. "My sister had the same thing. When she passed away, I found she had a box of 30 watches in her closet. I understood right away!"

Very often, these people have found that there seems to be a connection between these events and how they are feeling. When they are feeling stressed or angry, their emotions appear to interfere with electronics around them. "I noticed it happens more often when I am stressed," Kamilla says. "I wish there was a pill to make it go away."

* Circling back to invisibility cloaking, then, my view is that it's all about the manipulation of energy and a resulting trick of light. Our close cousins do not step into another dimension when they disappear any more than *we*, or any other animal, can. My trusted friend—the woman I call No-Bite in Part 1— once saw a Sasquatch crossing the road in front of her in broad daylight, and *before* it reached the cover of the trees, it simply disappeared. The passenger in her car saw the exact same thing. But just because the figure employed this rare adaptation, this defense mechanism, there is no reason whatsoever to use magical thinking to jump to the conclusion that he was no longer *present* before them. As Robin puts it, "They're still there, it's just that you can't see them. They're still just as physically there as you and I. Maybe they change their vibration; there's so many theories on how they disappear, but I know they do. I've seen it happen hundreds of times."

My proposed EMF explanation draws from the work of scientists who have been able to render objects invisible in the lab. For example, at the University of Toronto, Professor George Eleftheriades, PhD, and his co-author Michael Selvanayagam, have cloaked an aluminum cylinder using one layer of EMF-emitting antennas. The system can be scaled up to cloak larger objects using more loops, and the loops can become printed and flat, like a blanket or skin—or Sasquatch hair cover? By surrounding an object with small antennas that collectively radiate an EMF, like noise-cancelling headphones in the case of acoustics, the radiated field cancels out any light waves scattering off the cloaked object.

** MJR was in court, of all places, when his mood started to have its effects. "When I am angry or have gotten into an altercation, it appears to bring this on quickly," he says. "I was in court with my ex-wife. Needless to say, she was stating lies to the judge. The judge seemed to be eating this up. This made me so angry. There was a lamp sitting on the desk next to my attorney and me. When I seemed to have reached my peak anger, the light on the lamp went very bright and then started flickering erratically."

* In their paper, "Experimental demonstration of active electromagnetic cloaking,"[2] they explain that "We've taken an electrical engineering approach, and that's what we are excited about. It's very practical." Picture a mailbox sitting on the street. When light hits the mailbox and bounces back into your eyes, you see the mailbox. If we wrap the mailbox in the right frequency of EMF, this will cancel out any waves that would otherwise bounce back. In this way, surrounded by the field, the mailbox becomes undetectable.

Steering light around or away from a region of space—an object—to make it look as if it weren't there is called *transformation optics*. This term was coined in 1861 in the context of James Clerk Maxwell's revolutionary equations that describe the behavior of light as it passes through space. These equations form the foundation of the study of electromagnetism, classical optics, and electric circuits.

On the TEDx Talks YouTube channel, see Dr. Eleftheriades's fascinating presentation entitled "Extreme manipulation of electromagnetic waves with metamaterials," especially from 10:29 onward.

** Brenda's experience includes pain. "When I get emotionally upset or I am in a lot of pain, light bulbs burn out when I walk past them," she says. "One time I was at the mall in a lot of pain. I stopped to watch this man working on a model airplane that had an engine. As soon as I stopped to watch him, the motor came on and made the man jump out of his chair."

"For me, whenever I was scared, that's when I was releasing the most energy," Colada says. "One website I found said that I needed to figure out a way to mentally ground the energy or to calm myself during these times. So now, whenever I turn on lights in dark rooms, I release a slow breath of air and flick on the light switch at the same time. Since I started doing this, I have gone from burning out one bulb every other day, to one every six months or more."

Depression can also be a trigger, according to Bradly. "It started when I was nine," he says. "I used to pass by certain lights when I'd walk at night, and whenever I'd walk under them, they'd glow an eerie fluorescent blue and then blink out, so I thought they were haunted. Since I am a manic-depressive, whenever I was down the interference would seem to happen randomly and without warning, which would really spook me.

On the other side of the coin, Breezeq says it happens when she's happy. "It won't happen for a few days, then—bam!—if I'm driving super happy, street lights turn off or on just as I'm driving under them. Driving home tonight, three lights went out. There's no way this is a coincidence, not this regularly!"

One of the most annoying aspects of this affliction is that it can get downright expensive when just about every piece of electronics you touch gets destroyed. "I break every pair of headphones I wear," says Josh. "I break every printer I use just by printing on it, and cell phones never last more than a few months before they are corrupted."

Besides ringing up the expense of having to constantly replace watches, light bulbs, computers, and other valuables, this effect can be troublesome and embarrassing, especially in public. "Last March, I had got the wrong shoes and took them back," Tonya says, "and when the cashier tried to open her register, it would not budge. A second person came over and still could not get the drawer to open. A manager came and the

---

**thing would not open, and they were wondering what was wrong with the register. I walked off to get something and I heard it open as soon as I walked away. I told them I have that kind of effect on electronics. I have zapped computers, and restaurant signs have shut off around me only to come back on when I leave."

More than just embarrassment, this problem can have devastating effects on the job. "My older brother once worked for the state as a computer programmer," says Nightshade, who also affirms it runs in the family. "One night working third shift with the state's mainframes, he patted the mainframe and jokingly and told it, 'Go to sleep.' The state's entire computer network shut down for 24 hours. The fault was eventually tracked down to the mainframe my brother had touched."

Chad suspects it was a car accident in his youth that brought about his abilities. "I was in a bad wreck when I was seven," he says, "and I have read that traumatic experiences can have an effect on individuals and their brains in a positive and or a negative way. When I was eight, I began to notice that street lights would go out as I was walking down the sidewalk."

Then Chad realized he could control it to a certain degree. "Ten years ago, I noticed I could shut off lights while meditating," he says. "I can even manipulate these lights at a distance. The farthest has been a half mile away. I hold my arm out and begin to concentrate on the light, then I begin to feel the heat in the palm of my hand, and as I concentrate the heat intensifies, the lights begin dimming, and after approximately 20 seconds, the light turns off. I started meditating over a decade ago and I believe I have been able to 'exercise' my ability and effectively concentrate it, and now direct it."*** (Article by Stephen Wagner)

***It seems Chad may have some Sasquatch in his family tree!

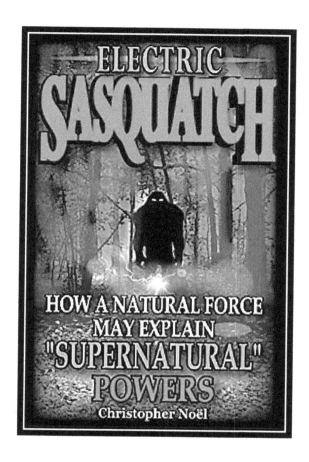

Part 3
Experimental Evidence

Beyond Magical Thinking

In the long history of human inquiry, magical thinking seems to be a phase that we must pass through on our way to a more rational, granular, and verifiable form of knowing. Lightning bolts were "known," in ancient Greece, to be hurled Earthward by Zeus. Mental illness and seizures were once interpreted, in many cultures, as demonic possession. The catalogue of old-school errors could go on and on.

In our own contemporary effort to comprehend the Sasquatch species, many seek to reduce and simplify the case by accepting supernatural "explanations" such as inter-dimensional travel through portals, extraterrestrial ("star people") origins and powers, biblical reportage about "giants in the earth" sired by angels, etc. In the future, when we look back at these concepts, I suspect that we will place them in the same class as all of the other attractive conceptual shortcuts that fill the annals of the history of science in earlier centuries and that give way, inevitably, to a more accurately grounded understanding.

Sasquatch research still stands where chemistry stood in the late Renaissance — halfway between alchemy and empirical realism. Nature can be very protective of her secrets, and in the face of mystery, we tend first to stubbornly avoid the laborious, tedious work of the scientific method and opt instead for the route of less resistance.

Like an awkward bout of mindspeak, I can hear you laughing at the irony: Here I am looking down my nose at magical thinking in the midst of a book in which I embrace mind reading. Fair enough, but of course the whole point is that this phenomenon is not magical at all but, I'm insisting, a natural ability that has been demonstrated in human experience generally and, specifically, in the case of our interactions with Sasquatch. I'm convinced by my own firsthand experiences in East Texas and by the several dozen incidents presented in Part 2; indeed, any *one* of these would suffice, for, as Dutch psychiatrist Frederik van Eeden wrote, "All science is empirical science; all theory is subordinate to perception; a single fact can overturn an entire system."

My next challenge, here in Part 3, is to build a bridge between these real-world episodes and the much more deliberative and rigorous assessment that has taken place — with little fanfare and much knee-jerk opposition — in the arena of controlled experimentation. In other words, yes, contrary to popular opinion, there exists a critical mass of persuasive evidence for the legitimacy of telepathy stretching back more than a century. By hundreds of credible scientists, "unbelievable" claims have been put to the test.

So let us now turn from magic to measurement, from personal stories to laboratories.*

---

*Here in Part 3, I will not include a high level of detail and complexity. For readers wishing to delve more deeply into the nature and history of parapsychological research, I recommend the following resources.

Basic Experiments in Parapsychology, K.R. Rao, 1984.
Rao includes thirteen experimental reports and seven review articles involving meta-analysis and the assessment of evidence in specific areas of psychic research. The author provides a representative sample of the extensive literature in the field of parapsychology and presents a few basic experiments illustrating various procedures and broadly reflecting the major trends of this field of research.

Mind-Reach: Scientists Look at Psychic Abilities, Harold E. Puthoff and Russell Targ, Eds., 1977.
This book is a clear, straightforward account of a set of successful experiments that demonstrate the existence of "remote viewing," a hitherto unvalidated human capacity. It is a regular piece of scientific work, as is the study of communication among bees or the luminescence of fireflies. Contemporary quantum physics, specific qualities of electromagnetic fields, and advances in brain research not only have determined the experimental methods but have also contributed to the tentative explanations advanced in this book as to how this newly observed ability might operate. (from the Introduction by Margaret Mead)

The Reality of ESP: A Physicist's Proof of Psychic Abilities, Russell Targ, 2012.
"If facts alone can convince a skeptical investigator of the reality of ESP, this book should do it," writes physicist Russell Targ, pioneer in the development of the laser and laser applications. He and his colleagues have demonstrated beyond reasonable doubt that the mind can function without limitation in space and time and that this ability is teachable and practical. Believing that most of us have psychic abilities we haven't tapped, Targ describes how we can learn to develop them, simply by working at home with a friend.

Phenomena: The Secret History of the U.S. Government's Investigation into Extrasensory Perception and Psychokinesis, Annie Jacobson, 2017.
For more than forty years, the U.S. government has researched extrasensory perception, using it in attempts to locate hostages, fugitives, secret bases, and downed fighter jets, and to divine other nations' secrets. The agencies involved include the CIA, NSA, DEA, the Navy, Air Force, and Army. [For a TED Talk overview, see YouTube under "Russell Targ Stanford Research Institute."]

Entangled Minds: Extrasensory Perception in a Quantum Reality, Dean Radin, 2006.
Radin shows how we know that psychic phenomena such as telepathy, clairvoyance, and psychokinesis are real, based on scientific evidence from thousands of controlled laboratory tests. And then, he entertains ways in which the theory of quantum physics may allow for a greater understanding of these abilities.

For an introduction to Radin's approach to matters surrounding psychic research, see YouTube: "Science and the taboo of psi."

Senders and Receivers

Picture a room that looks like a large walk-in freezer but warm and with a comfortable chair — a solid steel, double-walled chamber that shields against electromagnetic signals and acoustic noise. Now picture another room, fifty feet away within the same building and containing another chair and a computer screen. The sender (S) sits in front of the screen. The receiver (R) sits in the isolation chamber; all she has to work with are four picture cards showing, say, a horse, a pair of scissors, a mountain, and a car. Ten times during a thirty-minute sending session, S is shown a randomly selected image (one of the four) on the screen and attempts to mentally convey it to R. R is simultaneously instructed to envision the "target" image and then make her best guess.

By pure chance, R should score a "hit," select the correct card, 25% of the time.

According to Dean Radin, author of *Entangled Minds*, between 1974 and 2004 a total of eighty-eight experiments following this basic template were performed (sometimes substituting video clips for still images and entailing other small variations), reporting 1008 hits in 3145 trials for a combined hit rate of 32%. This 7% above-chance effect represents an *unlikelihood* of 29,000,000,000,000,000,000 to 1. Unlikelihood is technically known as "odds against chance."[3]

The Sense of Being Stared At

This phenomenon has been experimentally investigated for nearly a century. In the typical set-up, two people sit within ten yards of one another, R with her back to S. S flips a coin to determine whether or not to stare at the back of R's head. If the assignment is to stare, then for ten seconds, S stares intensely at R, then the experimenter alerts R with a clicking tone to respond either "yes" or "no." Each one of these attempts is called a *trial*.

British biologist Rupert Sheldrake has conducted numerous experiments based on this simple design. Radin has conducted a meta-analysis of sixty such experiments by Sheldrake and others involving a total of 33,357 trials and found that the overall success rate is 54.5%, whereas the chance expectation is, of course, 50%. The odds against chance for this result are 202

octodecillion to 1, or 202,000,000,000,000,000,000,000,000,
000,000,000,000,000,000,000,000,000,000,000 to 1.[4]

(See Sheldrake's YouTube lecture "The Extended
Mind: Recent Experimental Evidence." And for a much
more comprehensive discussion, see his article "The Sense
of Being Stared At" in the *Journal of Consciousness Studies*
12, 2005, and his 2013 book by the same title.)

This staggering against-chance ratio is a great deal
larger than the one reported for the image-sending
experiment above. This is due to the nearly eleven-fold
higher total trials here, 33,357, as opposed to just 3145 for
the image-sending experiment.

A word about statistical significance. Anyone can
readily tell that 7% represents a healthy chunk of 25%; so
does 4.5% of 50%. We'll soon see, however, that in
parapsychological studies — even those with "successful"
outcomes — the margins are typically *much* narrower. One
persistent obstacle in persuading skeptics of the validity of
psychic phenomena is that they stubbornly hold out for
"slam dunk" results, rather like Sasquatch skeptics
demanding a body on a slab. Unfortunately, the nature of
extrasensory perception is such that it is far from perfectly
reliable; even the most robust findings, such as the two just
cited, include many "misses" — 68% in the first and 45.5%
in the second. It's by analyzing the ratio of hits to misses,
and then assessing this against the background of pure
chance, that we can assess significance.

Looking across a whole range of test results from
blatant to subtle, a guy who knew a thing or two about
numbers, Alan Turing, declared that "the statistical
evidence for telepathy is overwhelming."[5]

In the next two experiments, the results are much quieter but no less relevant to the topic of this book and are indeed supportive of many of the experiences related in Parts 1 and 2.

Reach Out and Touch Someone

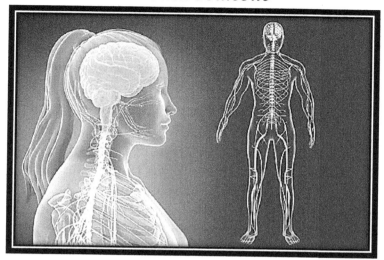

In parapsychology, DMILS refers to "direct mental interaction with living systems." Can one subject consciously influence, from a distance, the physical sensations or processes of another? Here, too, many trained professionals have designed experiments to plumb this mystery.

R is seated in a comfortable reclining chair within the standard isolation chamber and wired up with sensors that measure her skin's sweat output, a time-tested gauge of a person's autonomic nervous system and emotional state.

S is seated in a distant, also insulated room in front of a video monitor and asked to follow instructions that pop up on the screen. At random, he is prompted to either *calm* R or *activate* her. If the former, he might imagine her relaxing on a beach. If the latter, she's skydiving or being chased up a steep hill. Over the course of thirty minutes, the computer is programmed to call at random for twenty *calms** and twenty *activates*.

Afterward, the investigator has the continuous read-out of R's skin conductance data to juxtapose against S's series of instructions.

In 2004, psychologist Stefan Schmidt and his colleagues at the University of Freiburg Hospital, Germany, published a meta-analysis of DMILS research in the *British Journal of Psychology*.[6] They found forty soundly conducted studies between 1977 and 2000, reporting 1055 sessions (not trials this time but entire sessions). Setting a random value for hits vs. misses at 50%, the overall hit rate was a gravely disappointing 50.7%. We can almost hear the descending cascade of trombone notes. But wait — statistics to the rescue. Given the sheer number of trials contained within these 1055 sessions, what we arrive at is that this 50.7% represents a surprising 2000 to 1 odds against chance, which is still easily steep enough to humble any genuinely open-minded skeptic, if any such there be.

---

*Recall Denise in Maine (Part 2): "I'm getting overwhelmed, and it's like she's very attuned to me, and when she realizes she is doing that, she makes me feel calm so she can continue. She sensed that I was getting too much energy from her."

Entangled Minds

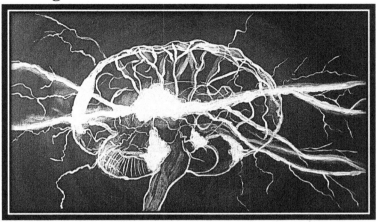

Another important category of DMILS experiment — and one that also relates directly back to the experiences shared in Parts 1 and 2 — seeks to measure a connection between two individuals, but this time an involuntary one.

The design used here asks, in effect, whether poking one person will produce an *ouch* in a distant partner — like when I gave Nantaya the cheese cake and the next morning No-Bite felt the sugar headache. The "poke" is a stimulus like a flashing light to cause one of the brains to "jump" electrically, as detected via EEG.

Below, a positive result is depicted within a 2014 study conducted by University of Edinburgh psychologists Marios Kittenis, Peter Caryl, and Paul Stevens.[7] Both S and R were placed inside a pitch-dark Functional MRI scanner so that their visual cortexes (at the back of the brain) could be precisely monitored. At random intervals, a light would flash in S's eyes, which would cause his or her visual cortex to react strongly. In the top row, this

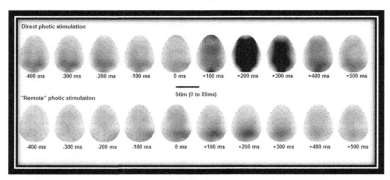

reaction can be seen in the sixth, seventh, and eighth snapshots. Meanwhile, in the bottom row, the brain of R, who is shown no light flash but is concentrating on S, responds weakly yet unmistakably. This result was obtained often enough to constitute an odds against chance of 50 to 1. Importantly, a control group was also scanned inside the dark tube for the same length of time but (unbeknownst to them) paired with no corresponding S. R was alone in these one-sided trials and *never once* displayed any such visual cortex response.

Leanna Standish and colleagues at Bastyr University, Washington State, conducted a similar EEG correlation experiment[8] in which S and R were located, again, inside an fMRI scanner. The experimenters first auditioned thirty pairs of people to find one that was able to produce a correlation more consistently than the others.

Testing the chosen couple in the official final run, then, they found a highly significant increase in brain activity in R's visual cortex while the distant partner was viewing a flickering light at random intervals.

What was this "highly significant increase"? Five out of sixty. That is, eleven out of every twelve times S was shown a flickering light, R's brain showed no response whatsoever. That is, the misses far outweighed the hits. But keep in mind that, lying in the pitch-dark fMRI scanner, R's visual cortex had no cause to respond this way *at all*, much less five times. As Standish has said, "If it happens even *once*, that's kind of amazing."

Remember as well that we're talking about the one pair that, out of thirty, had pretested positive for above-average connectedness; think how much worse the others would've done.

We're beginning to catch on to the inherent subtlety and nuance of statistical analysis. Nothing about it manages to bash us over the head with the kind of immediacy and drama described in Parts 1 and 2. Why is this?

Consider the importance of context. On the one hand, we have a sterile laboratory setting and participants asked to perform tricks, on command, under the watchful eye of scientists and machines. On the other hand, we have one's natural environment, one's most intimate local landscape playing host to years of repeated routines, reinforced behavior, and familiar thought patterns.

Now add to the mix the evidently much greater proficiency of the Sasquatch species than our own when it comes to connecting mentally and emotionally on a higher level…and we're good to go. Home world beats formal laboratory conditions every time—to say nothing of a lab staged on national television.

Uri Geller

These days, if people remember him at all, it's usually for his disastrous 1973 appearance on *The Tonight Show*. Geller had earned by then a worldwide following for his feats of telepathy and psychokinesis (primarily the bending of keys and spoons).

Before the interview, Carson's producers had shown their guest a list of questions he'd be asked. Instead, what greeted him was a tableful of paraphernalia Geller had previously used to establish his abilities. Feeling ambushed and thrown off balance by this procedural sleight-of-hand, he found himself unable to perform. The YouTube video is painful to watch: "Uri Geller on The Tonight Show (Full)."

As we've learned above, though, extrasensory functioning is anything but automatic; it's subject to all the same fallibilities and fluctuations inherent in the human animal, which are then of course compounded when one is put on the spot in front of millions of television viewers — devotees and skeptics alike. Not understanding this, however, detractors promptly leapt upon the "failure" as proof of Geller's fraudulence; his reputation took a hit from which it has never fully recovered.

I'm going to simply lay all that aside because this man is an important figure in the history of our subject. Geller first came to the attention of the U.S. government in the late 1960s; declassified documents show that CIA analysts became intrigued and concerned by his capacity for "mind projection" in which he could "force" a person to name, with a startling degree of accuracy, a city he'd earlier written down. If indeed it was possible for a person to implant a thought in another's mind, could remote behavior control be far behind? This concept had clear national security implications.

Please offset the Carson video with this one: "Secret CIA Psychic Lab Experiments with Uri Geller at Stanford University." Here, you'll see him operating in his comfort zone, confident and willing, among his research partners at the Stanford Research Institute, or SRI. The most impressive segments of this documentary, in my view, are those in which his success rates represent astronomical odds against chance. He is able to 1. draw pictures that closely resemble those that are double-sealed inside envelopes; 2. choose the one steel canister, among many, that contains a ball bearing or water; and 3. divine where, inside a shaken box, a die has landed and which of its six sides is facing up.

SRI forms the core of Annie Jacobsen's comprehensive 2017 book, *Phenomena: The Secret History of the U.S. Government's Investigations into Extrasensory Perception and Psychokinesis*. Jacobsen is a National Book Award finalist and an assiduous researcher. These 526 pages are a treasure trove for anyone interested not only in psychic prowess generally but also in its bizarre, erratic journey through the halls of political power, both in the United States and in the Soviet Union.

In the SRI video recommended above, you'll observe that from 16:10 to 24:10, Geller's manipulation of matter without touching it—altering the weight of a one-gram metal object on a super-sensitive electrical scale and causing a compass needle to move—suggests the possible involvement of some form of electromagnetic energy. Furthermore, in *Phenomena*, Jacobsen writes that

> Scientists and researchers working with Geller at SRI reported that both inside and outside the lab, strange things sometimes occurred. Otherwise reliable equipment malfunctioned when he was around. Computers crashed. Magnetic tape became demagnetized.[9]

We note immediately the parallels here to the material included in the footnotes at the end of Part 2—a striking similarity to other cases of "electric people," to the experience of being zapped by Sasquatch, and to the "Bigfoot curse" encountered by field researchers in which their electronic gear becomes temporarily disabled.

How might we interpret this pregnant yet evasive connection? Well, it could certainly turn out to be the case that the highly developed Sasquatch faculties, mindspeak included, bear some elemental relationship with the electromagnetic spectrum. After all, there are only four known forces in nature—the strong and weak nuclear forces, gravity, and electromagnetism—so it seems reasonable to suppose that *any* natural phenomenon, or cluster of phenomena, that involve energy will arise from one of these fundamental sources. At least, should we not explore and exhaust the potential insights already available "on the books" before resorting to more far-fetched explanations that reach "off book"?

The resonance between psychic research and human-Sasquatch interaction continues even a bit further, as well. In the winter of 1975, Geller was studied by nuclear physicists at the Lawrence Livermore National Laboratory in Berkeley, California. They ran experiments—not yet fully declassified—that tested whether he could mentally interfere with laser beams and/or computer program cards sealed inside a lead container. He was able to erase the magnetic pattern stored on the cards, but that is the only publicly known result.

Of more import for our purposes is the fact that several of these researchers experienced something akin to what's commonly associated with Sasquatch habituation sites and field research.

> Each morning, in keeping with nuclear clearance protocols, the scientists were required to report anything unusual that had happened overnight. After the second day of tests, security officer Ron Robertson called Kit Green at CIA headquarters. "He told me there was a serious problem," recalls Green [in a 2015 interview conducted by Jacobsen].

Several of the nuclear weapons engineers had reported seeing things they could not rationally explain. These included "lights flashing in their rooms, a six-inch ball of light rolling down a hallway, and a flying orb."[10]

Curiously, the physicists didn't see these manifestations in Geller's direct presence but only later, in a separate space. Given that more than one man reported flashes and spheres of light, it seems that they were *influenced* to envision them, and then the question becomes, Why? Why these images in particular?

All we can say is that between Geller's energy work — like affecting a compass — and these nighttime visions, the common denominator seems to be the electromagnetic spectrum. And this aspect of nature has been, I've learned, a suspected medium of extrasensory perception for 150 years, ever since Heinrich Hertz demonstrated the existence of radio waves in 1886 and, soon after, Marconi first successfully transmitted a radio signal across the Atlantic Ocean.

Indeed, the radio is a useful metaphor for telepathic communication. Upton Sinclair's 1930 book, *Mental Radio*, chronicled his and his wife's experiments; she was able to tune in to and reproduce, to a remarkable degree of accuracy, drawings that Sinclair made elsewhere. Albert Einstein found that the book "deserves the most earnest consideration. The results of the telepathic experiments carefully and plainly set forth stand surely far beyond those that a nature investigator holds to be conceivable."[11]

The metaphor is limited, however, by the fact that radio waves, and most other frequencies on the spectrum, cannot penetrate lead or the mesh of metals that make up an EMF-blocking "Faraday cage." In the 1940s, researchers Puharich and Hammond found that placing psychics inside such an enclosure did not reduce their capacity to perform telepathy at rates above chance. And, of course, we've seen that recent experiments routinely employ lead-lined chambers.

In other words, it seems that the electromagnetic spectrum is not likely to be the explanatory key to extrasensory perception.

Remote Viewing

You may recall that what really caught my attention first, in East Texas, 2011, was that the resident Sasquatch, Nantaya, was able to accurately envision my research area back in northern Vermont — my "dirt bridge," etc. — some seventeen hundred miles away.

It turns out that some of our own species can do this, too, and that the practice of "remote viewing" has enjoyed a favored place in parapsychological research for many years. The main name you need to know here is Russell Targ, a physicist and pioneer in the development of the laser in the 1940s and co-founder of the Stanford Research Institute in 1972. If you find yourself intrigued by the concept of remote viewing, drop everything, grab some popcorn, and watch two videos — first, a recent interview with Targ on YouTube called "Third Eye Spies with Russell Targ," and then the brand-new documentary itself, which is now available to stream on Vimeo and Amazon Prime. For decades, Targ has sought to get his former colleagues on record discussing their long-secret collective work in the 1970s and 80s. This documentary represents the culmination of these efforts, finally released just shy of Targ's eighty-fifth birthday.

In the interview, Targ asserts that remote viewing is a natural human ability, that anyone can be trained "to quiet the mind" and fulfill a targeted mental outreach; it's just a matter of learning to tell the difference between images that derive from one's own unconscious and those that are implanted from an external source. Recall Elizabeth's and Robin's testimonials, in Part 2, in which they emphasize the difficulty, at times, of distinguishing between self and other in the case of thoughts, images, and voices. "The unasked-for, surprising image," Targ explains,

> is a key. You see, a problem with doing ESP
> experiments is that things that people
> imagine do not have a little tag on them
> saying, "This image is brought to you by

ESP." That would be very nice. I've now got years of experience as an interviewer, talking to people, helping them pull out of their unconscious the true psychic image as compared with the noise. In engineering terms, you'd say that ESP is a signal-to-noise problem. I can help them because my experience and discernment help them tell what's psychic and what's not.[12]

This relates to our earlier recognition that psychic performance is hindered by the ordinary pitfalls of any difficult endeavor — what Targ is calling "noise" in the system.

As leader of the SRI remote viewing project, Targ oversaw numerous iterations of the same basic experiment. Two researchers, called the *outbounder team*, would begin their day at SRI. They'd randomly choose an envelope from a group of sealed envenlopes kept in a safe. The team (S) would leave the office and, once inside their vehicle, open the sealed envelope, which contained a photograph of a nearby landmark with an address written underneath. Destinations included the courtyard of the Stanford Museum, the exterior of the Palo Alto City Hall, the local public tennis courts, etc. S would drive to the target site and wait there until a predetermined time, at which point they would survey the place with concentration, mentally recording the details. At the same time, R, sitting inside an isolation chamber, would sketch what he perceived S was sending him telepathically.

After training team members in such outbounder practice and obtaining positive results, the program evolved to pursue its government-mandated missions. Of the many striking hits I could relay here, I'll pick just one — the famous case of the Russian submarine.

Members of the National Security Council had been shown photograps taken by a KH-9 spy satellite that revealed a massive building at the Severodvinsk Naval Base in Russia. Located 650 miles north of Moscow near the Arctic Circle, this base was under high suspicion by the U.S. intelligence community because of a sudden uptick in activity at the site.

In Remote Viewing Session C54, a sealed envelope was placed on a table in front of SRI remote viewer Joe McMoneagle. He was asked to provide information about the photo hidden inside. McMoneagle described a huge building "near some kind of shoreline, either a big lake or some bay. It smells like a gas plant, he said, "like there's smelting or melting going on inside the building." He mentioned

> lots of people in funny hats…arc welding activity…standing on catwalks. They're cutting metal or bending metal, welding metal, shaping metal. Very, very large. There's some kind of ship. Some kind of vessel. I'm getting a very strong impression of propellers. Jesus! This is really mind blowing. I'm seeing fins, but they're not rocket fins or airplane fins. They're…they look like *shark* fins. I'm getting a stong impression of a huge, coffin-type container. It's like they created part of a submarine to…to fasten this modification to. I think it's like a prototype, perhaps four, five, or six stories tall. I'm asking myself the question, What is this thing? This coffin-like thing?

And the answer I keep getting is that it's a weapon.[13]

McMoneagle added that he saw "a concrete structure, like a canal in Holland."

That the Soviets would build a submarine inside this building, and not in a dry dock located at the water's edge, seemed to defy logic. The building in the picture was roughly one hundred yards from the shore at the naval yard, nor was any canal visible — only flat, frozen earth.

Four months after this session, however, new images captured by the satellite over Severodvinsk sent shock waves through the intelligence community. They revealed a massive submarine tethered alongside a dock as well as a channel that had evidently been recently dynamited between the building and the dock. It was now clear that the Soviets had covertly constructed a prototype for an entirely new generation of nuclear-powered, ballistic missile submarines. The Russian code name was *акула*, which translates to *shark*.

Severodvinsk Naval Base

Adventures in the Hive Mind

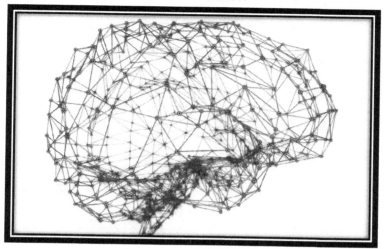

I've wondered which is more likely, that Nantaya was able to key into my local landscape directly, when I asked for her help with my Vermont research, using her mind's eye alone, or that she was instead joining a network of interconnected subjectivities—those of her own kind living near me. Perhaps in his remote viewing, Joe McMoneagle tapped into Soviet personnel at the Severodvinsk Naval Base.

The concept of a *hive mind*, or *collective consciousness*, has a long history.[14] In his 1979 book *Lifetide: The Biology of the Unconscious*, South African zoologist and ethologist Lyall Watson pointed to behavior observed in macaque monkeys in the early 1950s on the island of Kōjima; adults learned to wash sweet potatoes and then passed this skill onto younger members of the group. This practice then somehow "spread" to neighboring islands, many miles apart, even though the species cannot swim.[15]

In 2011, blue tits in the UK taught themselves to break into milk bottles and drink the cream at the top. The species soon exhibited the same newly acquired skills in other countries throughout Europe and Asia. This was despite the groups' never meeting—these birds are non-migratory.[16]

Speaking of birds, some believe that the astonishingly fluid and coordinated *murmuration* of starling flocks represents collective consciousness at work, in that the dance is never led by a single individual but governed equally by all members, working together.

These and other similar cases do not, of course, constitute hard scientific proof of parapsychological communication, but they are certainly suggestive. To me, it makes sense that if telepathy is genuine — which we now know that it is — then something akin to the notion of a hive mind or communal awareness is implied. Why?

1. Telepathy is apparently not affected by distance, as shown by the Stanford Research Institute, my experience in Texas and Vermont, and by Wayne's and Todd's in Alaska and Michigan; recall their simultaneous onslaught, five thousand miles apart, of "moaning and wailing."

2. Therefore, all minds everywhere should be, in principle, equally accessible — if they are, so to speak, "on line."

One sustained effort to measure a human hive mind effect is the Global Consciousness Project, administered by Roger Nelson out of Princeton University. At seventy spots around the world, the GCP has stationed random number generators or RNGs — electronic "coin-flippers" that generate thousands of results (either 0 or 1) per second. On their website, the GCP explains that when left alone, these machines

> show no significant pattern. But when a great event synchronizes the feelings of millions of people, our network of RNGs becomes subtly structured. The probability is less than one in a billion that the effect is due to chance. The evidence suggests a unifying field of consciousness.

Our purpose is to examine subtle correlations that reflect the presence and activity of consciousness in the world. The data overall show a highly significant departure from random expectation in coordination with certain globally relevant events.[17]

In *Entangled Minds*, Radin runs through several of the GCP's more noteworthy results[17], points in time at which the random flow of worldwide data suddenly displayed a striking degree of order. I'll cover just a couple before we move on, in Part 4, to investigate how both one-on-one telepathy and mass manifestations like the hive mind may be illuminated by such quantum concepts as *nonlocality* and *entanglement*.

The live television broadcast of the funeral of Pope John Paul II, on April 8, 2005, was an event that captured the devoted attention of hundreds of millions of people around the world. Just beforehand, Roger Nelson predicted that the network of RNGs would show a significant deviation from the norm, and sure enough, the data shifted, acquiring a small but detectable dash of otherwise inexplicable order with odds against chance of 42 to 1.

Four and a half years earlier, something happened that elicited an even more intense emotional response from the human race. On the morning of September 11, 2001, the RNG data shifted into a state of increased patterning—an extremely unlikely and persistent temporal structure known as an *autocorrelation*, which is a measure of how similar data are over time as compared to ordinary baseline values. In the graph below, the black convergence of results in the lower half captures the identical analysis for the sixty days surrounding 9/11. The upper parabola represents odds against chance of one million to 1, and we can see that here is in fact where the 9/11 autocorrelation data lie. This effect lasted for eight hours before beginning to trail off. Note that *nobody was thinking about the RNGs themselves,* so this outcome is not an example of mind affecting matter intentionally and directly. Instead, what's suggested here is that the combined simultaneous worldwide focus upon one horrific event somehow resonated in such a manner as to add order, if only briefly, to a global information field that also included the RNGs' processes.

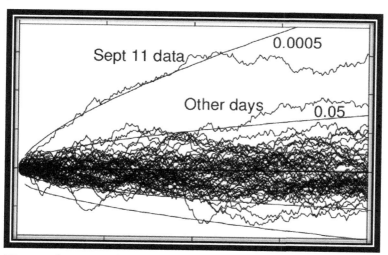

Degree of autocorrelation measured on 9/11 and surrounding days. Nothing remotely similar occurred during the other 364 days of 2001.

Part 4

How are Such Things Even Possible?

If telepathy is a real fact, it is very possible that it is operating at every moment and everywhere, but with too little intensity to be generally noticed. The atmosphere is continually electrified, we move among magnetic currents, yet millions of human beings lived for thousands of years without having suspected the existence of electricity. It may be the same with telepathy.

— Henri Bergson (1859-1941)

Telepathy has probably more to do with physics than with psychology.

— Albert Einstein

See, people don't think this stuff is real, but it's as real as it gets.

— Robin in South Carolina

Matter and Consciousness

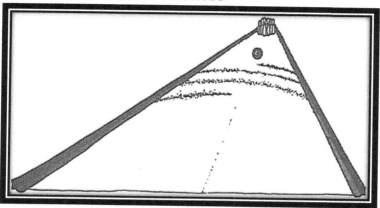

One of the key findings of quantum physics is that at the most fundamental level, matter's building blocks do not obey common-sense rules. For example, when they are observed and measured by us, elementary particles behave like discrete things—like a single bowling ball proceeding along a single path. But when they are *not* observed and measured, they behave very differently—like a series of *possible* bowling balls occupying a sweep of *possible* positions.

In *The Holographic Universe*, Michael Talbot writes,

> there is compelling evidence that the only
> time elementary particles (aka *quanta*) ever
> manifest as or coalesce into particles is when
> we are looking at them. This seems more like
> magic than the kind of behavior we are
> accustomed to expect from the natural world.
> Physicist Nick Herbert says that he sometimes
> imagines that behind his back the world is

always "a radically ambiguous and ceaselessly flowing soup." But whenever he turns around and tries to see the soup, his glance instantly freezes it and turns it back into ordinary reality. He believes this makes us a little like Midas, the legendary king who never knew the feel of silk or the caress of the human hand because everything he touched turned to gold. "Likewise," Herbert says, "humans can never experience the true texture of quantum reality, because everything we touch turns to matter."[19]

By "touch," he means "apply our consciousness to," and by "matter," he means matter in its familiar everyday state. It turns out that reality and consciousness are intimately related, as has become increasingly clear over the past ninety-five years thanks to experiments revealing the impact of the latter upon the former — otherwise known as the *observer effect*. The prime example is the double-slit experiment, which Richard Feynman called "the central mystery" of quantum physics. Briefly stated, this experiment shows that elementary particles — such as photons of light — will behave, like the bowling ball above, as individual objects in certain positions when observed and, when not, as a sea of wavelike potential positions, or *superposition*, all existing at once."*

---

* In deciding how to approach this issue, I've had to make tough choices about the degree of technical nuance to include. If you want more depth and detail at this point, please read the excellent overview at "Double-Slit Experiment" on Wikipedia. For a video presentation, see YouTube: "Double-Slit Experiment Explained, by Jim Al-Khalili."

It was because of such strangeness that consciousness "seemed, to the great discomfort of physicists, to force its way into early quantum theory," writes Philip Ball on BBC Earth.

> When this "observer effect" was first noticed by the pioneers, they were deeply troubled. It seemed to undermine the basic assumption behind all science: that there is an objective world out there, independent of us. If the way the world behaves depends on how — or *if* — we look at it, what can "reality" really mean?[20]

Since the birth of quantum physics early in the twentieth century, a debate has raged as to whether and precisely how consciousness and matter are related. Instead of sailing off into the realm of competing abstractions, though, let's spend a minute back on the firm ground of experimentation to see if, empirically, at some level, the relationship does exist.

Telekinesis refers to the effect of mind upon matter. Though that's not the prime subject of this book, it's adjacent because, if demonstrable, it (like telepathy) means that mental influence transcends the localized brain inside the skull.

In 1997, engineer Robert Jahn and his colleagues at the Princeton Engineering Anomalies Research Laboratory (PEAR Lab) published a review of twelve years of experiments investigating mind-matter interactions.[21] The trials involved more than one hundred volunteers who attempted to mentally influence RNGs. Participants tried to influence the outputs to drift *above* the chance-expected average (by aiming for 1s, say), or *below* chance, or to withdraw their mental attention entirely to allow the RNGs to behave normally in the baseline or control condition. See YouTube: "Princeton Mind-Matter Interaction Research."

Radin explains that

> Over these twelve years, the PEAR Lab team found that the outputs tended to match the directions that the participants intended. When they wished for high scores the RNG outputs drifted up, and when they wished for low scores the outputs drifted down.

> Recently, I have located 490 studies worldwide over many years comprising 1.1 billion randomly generated bits subjected to mental intention. The overall effect is small, but its odds against chance stand at 50,000 to 1.[22]

The graph below shows the divergence among baseline results (BL), high-intending results (HI), and low-intending results. We can see that the observers' intentions (or lack thereof) affect the outcomes in a manner that conventional science cannot yet explain. These results were found in single-subject trials. The influence was even more pronounced when bonded couples or groups of subjects worked together in attempting to affect outputs; see the earlier discussion of the hive mind.

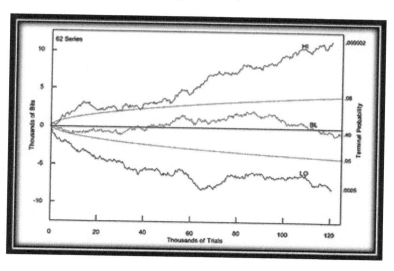

What are Nonlocality and Entanglement?

Nonlocality is the perfectly outrageous fact that, at bottom — within the quantum context — reality does not, so to speak, leave room for distance. Distance is an illusion, as is the notion that objects or places — such as Alaska and Michigan, Texas and Vermont — are located *here* or *there* in fixed positions independent of one another.

In the middle of the last century, physicists had to finally accept nonlocality after the discovery of a phenomenon known as *quantum entanglement*. This occurs when pairs or groups of particles — electrons, photons, etc. — are generated, interact, or share spatial proximity such that their states are then correlated no matter how far apart they may go. Measurements of physical properties such as position, momentum, spin, and polarization, performed on entangled particles, are found to be in perfect synch. For example, if one particle is found to have a clockwise spin on a certain axis, the spin of the other particle, measured on the same axis, will be found to be counterclockwise, and if the state of one is changed, the other's state will change as well — not quickly, not even at the speed of light, but *simultaneously*. This means that the two are not communicating but rather behaving as a single unit, like two sides of the same coin, irrespective of apparent distance.*

There is no *mechanism* that can account for entangled particles operating as one; they simply *do*, and this irreducible truth cannot be further analyzed in any traditional sense. As Radin puts it,

> Scientists have long assumed that the best way, indeed perhaps the *only* way, to understand something is to see how its pieces fit together. If we see an impressive clock and want to know what makes it tick, we take it apart. In medical research, the entire focus is on understanding a treatment's "mechanism of action." But quantum reality is holistic, and as such any attempt to study its

---

* To learn how this has been demonstrated, see YouTube: "Quantum Entanglement & Bell's Inequality Violation Verified by Alain Aspect" and "Quantum Entanglement Proved To Be Correct Even Billions Of Light-Years Away" at iflscience.com.

individual pieces will give an incomplete
picture.[23]

And that's the tricky part — to put it mildly. We have to
stretch our understanding to take on board the idea that
some natural phenomena just cannot be accounted for in
the ways we've always relied upon. Remember DMLS
("direct mental interaction with living systems")
experiments, cited in Part 3? After successfully conducting
one such, German EEG specialist Jiří Wackermann
lamented that "No biophysical mechanism is presently
known that could be responsible for the observed
correlations between the EEGs of two separated
subjects."[24]

In assessing telepathy, we're unlikely ever to find a
means of transmission, such as electromagnetic energy,
between "two separated subjects" because their
"separation" is an illusion. Let's try a simple analogy.

Is Mindspeak Fishy?

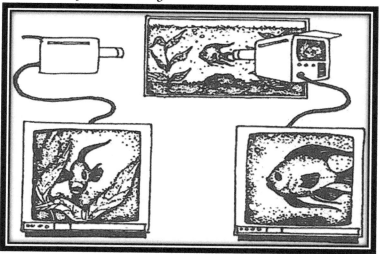

Picture an aquarium containing just one fish. Now imagine that you have never seen a fish or an aquarium before and your only knowledge of them comes from two video cameras, one aimed at the front of the tank and the other at the side. When you look at the two monitors, you'll assume that the fish on the screens are independent entities. But as you continue to watch, you will eventually realize that there must be some sort of relationship between the two fish. When one turns, the other makes a different but corresponding movement. You might assume that the two are simultaneously communicating or coordinating with one another, but this is not the case because, in fact, the "two" fish are one and the same.

This, essentially, is quantum reality, and it's about much more than entanglement between only two particles; it's about *connectedness* and *wholeness* more broadly. David Bohm (1917-1992) can help us here. He was one of the most influential theoretical physicists of the twentieth century and saw cohesion where others saw chaos or mere relational neutrality.

At the Berkeley Radiation Laboratory in the mid-1940s, Bohm began what was to become his landmark work on plasma. Plasma is one of the four fundamental states of matter, the others being solid, liquid, and gas. It can be generated by subjecting a neutral gas to a strong electromagnetic field, producing ions (electrically charged atoms). In *The Holographic Universe*, Talbot explains that Bohm was struck by how energy can become remarkably coherent under these conditions; it can be transformed into what he called "a state of quantum wholeness."

> Once they were in a plasma, electrons stopped behaving as individuals and started behaving as part of a larger and interconnected whole. Seemingly haphazard movements of individual electrons managed to produce highly organized overall effects. These were no longer situations involving just two particles, each behaving as if it knew what the other was doing, but entire oceans of particles, each behaving as if it knew what untold trillions of others were doing. Bohm remarked that he frequently had the impression the electron sea was "alive."[25]

In other words, it seems that electromagnetic energy can give rise to a state of matter — highly charged gas — that behaves in a coordinated fashion, like a massive flock of microscopic starlings in murmuration. Not only this, but plasma is strongly influenced by surrounding electromagnetic fields.*

And Bohm went much further than this. In the organized behavior of the plasma state, he saw a mirror of the "living" cosmos itself. In fact, he theorized that the entire universe is a single unified hologram.[26]

For the purposes of this book, the question we now face is this: How do we take the next step in comprehending telepathy within a quantum framework?

---

*   I'm reminded once again of the orbs that people see in association with Sasquatch activity. A recent breakthrough (2017) ties a similar phenomenon to plasma science: "Mystery of Ball Lightning Finally Solved: Eerie Orb-like Glow is Created when Radiation gets Trapped inside a Plasma Bubble." (DailyMail.co.uk) I suspect that Sasquatch can super-charge the air around them, producing areas of concentrated plasma energy, and can then manipulate these using electromagnetic fields. In less concentrated form, these EMFs are responsible for cloaking, zapping, disabling electronic equipment, etc.

Dean Radin explains that

> Quantum theory and a vast body of
> supporting experiments tell us that
> something unaccounted for is connecting
> otherwise isolated objects. And this is
> precisely what *psychic* experiences and
> experiments are telling us. The parallels are
> so striking as to suggest that psychic events
> are — literally — our subjective interface with
> quantum reality...with an internally
> coherent, nonlocal universe.[27]

In the spirit of Bohm, he gestures toward the primacy
of a high-order wholeness in marrying physics and
psychics.

> Quantum entanglement in elementary
> subatomic particles is, by itself, insufficient to
> explain telepathy and other psychic feats. But
> the parallels implied between entanglement
> and psychic experiences are too compelling
> to ignore. It's useful to ponder that if all we
> knew about reality were the behavior of
> atoms, nothing would suggest that living
> organisms would emerge when you put
> those atoms together in certain ways. Even
> less would we be able to predict the
> emergence of the complex phenomenon we
> call conscious awareness.[28]

The Right Receiver

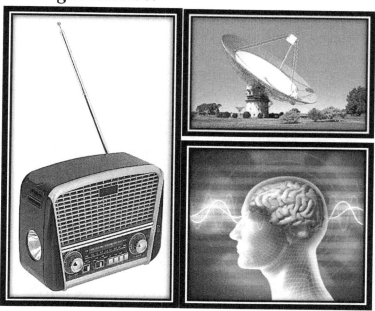

In our Internet Age, it's easy to take recent technological marvels for granted. To me, though, few things remain more remarkable than the simple radio. Switch one on and scan through the stations, settling on a good strong signal. Now take your radio along for a car ride into the countryside and pick out a distant hill or mountain. Park as near as possible and then climb to the top. Switch on your radio and hear the very same station, loud and clear. As far as the eye can see—and thousands of times farther—every square inch of open space perpetually contains the identical rich information, from singers to soliloquies to symphonies, in the form of extremely weak electromagnetic waves. The sheer disproportion between this weakness and the vast nuance it delivers draws our attention to the main miracle here—the design of the receiver.

Now step aside, sound, because unseen energy fields also transmit visual feasts. We could dwell on broadcast television, but that's nothing; NASA's New Horizons probe has sent back to Earth detailed images of Pluto— *more than three billion miles away*.

An astonishing level of surface detail is visible.

So how does this information reach us? The probe has two 12-watt radio transmitters.* To beam the signal to Earth, it uses a dish antenna 2.1 meters in diameter that works just like a rooftop satellite dish. Even then, by the time it arrives, the signal is ten thousand times too feeble to be detected by your home radio; it must be boosted by massive terrestrial antennas. Without these, it would be impossible to know or to prove that such a signal even existed. Again, once the signal is produced, it all comes down to the right kind of receiver to register and read it.

Apparently, when it comes to telepathic signals, our brains fit the bill at both ends. Thanks to millions of years of evolution, sender and receiver are compatible, but whatever the nature of this signal, it's either too weak or too ill-understood to fall within the wheelhouse of any current scientific instrument—by definition not properly designed.

Earlier, I explained how it is that, from a quantum perspective, we don't need to think of telepathy as the transmission of messages across spatial distance. Yes, they are messages, but they don't *travel*; instead, they *arise* within a unified and unifying information field.

The reason I touched on radios and the New Horizons probe is to emphasize the startling informational sufficiency of even vanishingly low levels of energy; in a nonlocal model of reality, as in classical Newtonian and post-Einsteinian models, energy in the system is needed to effect change, to cause such events as "He will do what he

---

*24 watts is not enough to power the dimmest incandescent light bulb.

must do" or "We are down by the river" or "Jessie!" And it's just *here* that electromagnetism likely enters the picture. Perhaps Sasquatch is better at telepathy than we are because — in addition to their presumably favorable brain anatomy — they have more access to and control over this energy source, which, as Henri Bergson put it long ago, "is operating at every moment and everywhere, but with too little intensity to be generally noticed."[29]

But how do our brains participate at the quantum level? Radin has an answer.

> Neurons communicate with each other through the release of neurotransmitter molecules. When an electrical signal reaches the end of a neuron, it causes channels in the neuron to open through which calcium ions can enter. If enough ions* are accumulated, the neuron releases neuro-transmitters, which in turn increase the tendency of brain neurons to "fire" their own electrical signals. Multiply that process by a few billion neurons and trillions of synapses, and that's the basic communication infrastructure of the brain.

---

* Interestingly, ions (charged particles) are also the fundamental constituents of coherent plasma balls; see p. 216 above.

> The quantum element enters at the ion
> channels, because at some points these
> channels are less than a nanometer in
> diameter, and at that size quantum effects
> become noticeable.[30]

Thanks to this right receiver of ours, infinitesimal signals can bestow rainbows of meaning. When in doubt, remember Pluto.*

---

*I recognize that it's difficult or impossible to hold in your mind, at the same time, two utterly divergent conceptions of reality. "Okay, so Pluto is three billion miles away and we can see it clearly with less than a lightbulb's worth of electric charge, but I thought distance is just an illusion..." True, at the quantum level, distance collapses and nonlocality takes over, and this is how and where telepathy is possible, but it's still the case that in other contexts distance is real. It's a very strange relationship between these two frameworks, I agree, if it can even be described as a "relationship" at all; you'll find as many ways to envision the issue as there are physicists. The Pluto example helps us only insofar as it vividly demonstrates how light a signal is required to accomplish a heavy informational payload, whether that information is propagated across vast Newtonian space or sparked within a quantum field.

The Intelligence of Things

Much to the delight of skeptics, Sasquatch are next to impossible to document on camera. Researchers have been long bewildered by the nearly 100% failure of trail cameras to obtain images or video of the species and have suggested explanations ranging from the machines' odor to their ultrasonic and infrared signals to their electromagnetic fields. All such mundane factors (especially the last) likely play a role, but it seems to me that the immaculate success of Sasquatch in confounding, decade after decade, even our most ingenious concealment efforts must point to some greater contribution. I think the missing piece of the puzzle is telepathy — this time between minds and *things*. In other words, not only can our next of kin proficiently avoid our attempts to capture their image with hand-held devices, but also, cameras left in the woods emit the very same invasive intention.

This is not a new idea, broadly speaking. We could go way back to Joseph Rodes Buchanan, who, in 1842, coined the term *psychometry* (measuring the soul) and proposed that "all things give off an emanation."

> The Past is entombed in the Present. The world is its own enduring monument. The discoveries of Psychometry will enable us to explore the history of man, as those of geology enable us to explore the history of the earth. There are mental fossils for psychologists as well as mineral fossils for the geologists.[31]

Current-day practitioners retain the name—*psychometrics*—for our mind's capacity to tap into an object's specific energy field. The chosen object transfers images and feelings regarding its history to the holder but can also portray tastes, smells, sounds, and even emotions to the more skilled or susceptible reader. Such a reader can glean strong psychic impressions that have been left behind by an object's previous owner or handler.

Not surprisingly, I'd like to place this concept within the quantum context. In "Do Inanimate Objects Have Thoughts and Feelings?", Tara MacIsaac presents the case quite well.

> The idea that the thermostat regulating the temperature in your house is even vaguely aware of what it is doing certainly goes against "common sense," wrote Henry P. Stapp, a theoretical physicist at the University of California–Berkeley who worked with some of the founding fathers of quantum mechanics. Nonetheless, he said, the idea of *panpsychism*—that all matter has

consciousness—is worth discussing in relation to quantum mechanics, where the link between mind and matter is so central that, he said, it is "rather unnatural anymore even to consider the possible existence of events that are not psycho-physical in character." The act of observation, an act of human consciousness, has been shown to influence the physical reality of experimental results. "Consciousness doesn't dangle outside the physical world as some kind of extra—it's there right at its heart."[32]

If panpsychism is indeed a genuine phenomenon, think of the implications. Consciousness shines through all, and the hive mind is far more pervasive than we first supposed.

Part 5
Links to Autism

Exposure Anxiety

An apparent paradox lies in the fact that, on the one hand, Sasquatch will do almost anything to avoid coming into immediate contact with us—instead, they *mediate* this contact in many ways—while, on the other hand, they will use mindspeak to reach us, and what could be a more direct and intimate form of communication?

For several years (see the next section), I have been thinking and writing about parallels between Sasquatch and autistic people—specifically autistic savants. One of the main features of autism is a syndrome called *exposure anxiety*, which autistic writer and psychologist Donna Williams describes in her book by that title. She covers the array of tactics used by those "on the spectrum" to evade direct interaction or confrontation with others. Williams's starting point is that autistic people tend to feel under constant threat of invasion by the chaotic outside world, and so they seek to protect themselves through precise daily routines, mental practices like memorization, repetitive behaviors—swaying, rocking, percussion, structuring their environment—and through maintaining sheer physical distance and concealment.

Of course, affinities with Sasquatch jump off the page, but my wish here is to unpack the significance within their different styles of being in the physical and the mental worlds.

In *Exposure Anxiety*, Williams explains that the priority in autistic life is the "building of a safe space, a foundation."[33] She writes that

> It's a myth that people with autism are not social. However aloof they are compelled to be, however diverting or outright retaliative they are in response to feelings of "invasion" and loss of control, these are the same people who will be a "fly on the wall," hovering in your space.[34]

She reflects on her own self-imposed childhood removal from the world of others, with its oppressive and constant danger.

> I responded best to an underplaying of interest. My father used to call me Spook because of the way I hovered about and then disappeared when approached—like a ghost.[35]

She further advises that the most effective means of "turning down the invasion-volume" in a person with exposure anxiety is to talk to them "through objects, interacting through an intermediary, [which] moves the focus off the person and onto the object/issue." Especially if this form of communication is practiced in "digestible small doses that leave the person wanting more, [it] can cause someone with exposure anxiety to" let down their guard a little.[36]

Sasquatch researchers and habituators know this approach only too well, having learned individually and collectively how much more effective is an "underplaying of interest" and the use of "objects [as] intermediar(ies)" than any more pressuring, heavy-handed approach.

"What is needed," writes Williams, and we can certainly agree in our own arena, "is the right and ability to *simply be* without being watched, studied, worked on, pursued. Just watch that your body language doesn't look focused on them and eagerly set to pounce."[37]

Above, Williams recalled that as a girl, she would both withdraw from her family and "hover about...like a ghost." She enjoyed being "a fly on the wall" — in touch yet also enclosed within a safety zone.

And in truth, what could be a more efficient means toward such invulnerable eavesdropping than telepathy, especially when it is *on your own terms,* as it seems to be for the Sasquatch communicators in Parts 1 and 2?

So, after all, there is no real paradox here. As long as you can be in charge, calling the shots, and sharing only what you decide to share, there is no peril. For autistic people, as for Sasquatch, the bottom line is *control;* allowable interaction must be "initiated and navigated by them."[38]

Very Special People

"Special" here is not intended as the condescending label that "normal" people sometimes like to apply to those with mental challenges such as Down syndrome, cerebral palsy, low-functioning autism, etc. Many misinterpret my theory, assuming it sees the Sasquatch species as suffering from a psychological handicap. Nothing could be further from the truth; instead of a disorder, I mean the opposite — a genius-level capacity for *order*, for precision, for memory, for tactical, strategic, analytical, and visual thinking akin to that of top chess players like autistic grandmaster David Navara, now ranked #18 in the world; or Daniel Tammet, author of *Born on a Blue Day*, who memorized pi to 22,514 digits; or Stephen Wiltshire, known as "the human camera," who, after just one helicopter flight over Rome, was able to reproduce the cityscape in exquisite detail.

See YouTube: "The Human Camera (Autistic Savant Documentary) —Real Stories."

Not all autistic people are such "prodigious savants," of course, but I'm arguing that, by nature, all Sasquatch are; otherwise, they wouldn't have been able to accomplish what they have for thousands of years and continue to accomplish daily. For example, a photographic (*eidetic*) memory would be indispensable in their enormously sophisticated project of survival and evasion, their perfect knowledge of the forest environment, their smooth and constant outmaneuvering of us across all landscapes—talk about three-dimensional chess to our checkers!

Autism is a highly heritable syndrome[39] with roots stretching deep into the past, and if it can run in families it can certainly run in a species. Neurobiologist John Harris writes that this "astonishing gift for visualization and pictorial thinking is an atavism—a re-expression or resurgence of an ancient style of thinking."[40]

My hypothesis is that our common ancestor in the primate family tree was endowed with a prototypical form of this cognitive prowess and that it has come down through our two evolutionary lines such that, today, we find differences in its manifestation and also striking similarities; for the latter, see YouTube: "The Sasquatch Savant Theory 1: Top 10 Parallels with Autism" or "The Mind of Sasquatch." For a full treatment of the theory, see the book pictured at the top of this section.

In a 2011 article published in the journal *Evolutionary Psychology*, Dr. Jaren Edward Reser sees autism as conferring a survival advantage; in other words, those occupying the spectrum today, though misfits in modern society, may owe their "symptoms" to a proud pedigree. Such people, Reser writes,

> are conceptualized here as ecologically competent individuals that could have been adept at learning and implementing hunting and gathering skills in the ancestral environment. For example, the obsessive, repetitive and systemizing tendencies in autism, which can be mistakenly applied toward activities such as block stacking today, may have been focused by hunger and thirst toward successful food procurement. Both solitary mammals and autistic individuals are low on measures of gregariousness, socialization, eye contact, facial expression, emotional engagement, affiliative need, and other social behaviors. The evolution of these neurological tendencies may hold important clues for the evolution of the autism spectrum and the natural selection of autism genes.[41]

And yet, one thing we know about current Sasquatch behavior is that they work together in coordinated groups; except in the case of rogue males, they're rarely solitary. Here, I think, is the main difference from human autistic expression. Whereas we, the further along the ASD spectrum we go, will shield ourselves more and more from direct contact with the Other (other people) and interact with them in a safely oblique, indirect manner, for Sasquatch the Other would seem to be *Homo sapiens* universally rather than members of their own group, and it is *us* whom they approach, when they do, in this same safely oblique, indirect manner.

So how does mindspeak fit in? I was interested to learn, not long ago, that autistic savants possess a much higher incidence of telepathic ability than the general population.[42] In our next three sections, we will explore this connection in some depth.

With Sasquatch, we're probably talking about a whole different social order from our own, one relying primarily on a type of "language" not written or voiced — perhaps far older than both — that promotes collective cohesion and tactical awareness.

But if Sasquatch can be in touch with one another effortlessly mind to mind, why not just remain forever incognito in the forest? Why all the loud and blatant wood knocks, these attention-grabbing whoops, screams, yells, and howls, which make a mockery of stealth by giving away both identity and location?

One day, in East Texas, I asked Nantaya this very question (through No-Bite). The answer came back immediately: "In mindspeak, we don't know where they are." That's all she'd share, but it was enough. Since telepathy is nonlocal, divorced from geography, it cannot help Sasquatch in practical operations on the ground, such as hunting or avoiding humans. It's like using a cell phone without GPS. Despite the risk involved, group positions must be announced and continually updated, nonlocal communication localized, sometimes subtly — tap tap tap — and sometimes not.

"Thank you, Nantaya," I said. "That makes sense." I started to raise the topic of quantum physics, but she wasn't interested.

"It Just Comes to Me"

Johns Hopkins-trained neuroscientist Diane Hennacy Powell, MD, is especially interested in autistic savants. She has focused on the kind of savant who is "able to provide information without any explanation for how they access it." In a recent interview[43], she recalls that

> they are not doing calculations in their head
> but the answer just pops into their
> consciousness. And they don't know how
> they get it. Often, such people cannot even do
> simple math, addition and subtraction, yet
> they can tell you what day of the week April
> 21, 1725 fell on. It just comes to them. This
> struck me as being quite similar to how
> answers spontaneously appear in the minds
> of people with psychic abilities. And in terms
> of brain function, this started to make sense
> to me.

We'll turn to the brain in the next section, but first I want to explore this link between telepathy and autistic savantism. Powell is not the only investigator to have noticed it. Pioneering researcher Darold Treffert included a section on extrasensory perception in these gifted people in his 1989 book, *Extraordinary People: Understanding Savant Syndrome*, and Bernard Rimland, who coined the term *autistic savant* in 1978, wrote case studies of precognition and other ESP abilities in autistic children.[44]

But nobody has pressed the issue like Powell, seeking out and directly assessing these remarkable individuals. About her most prominent recent research subject, she relates in the same interview cited above, that

> In August 2013, I learned of Hayley. She was eleven years old and had just recently started to say letters and numbers, but otherwise couldn't speak and still can't. She communicates with a keyboard. She also can't do simple math, but she can give the answers to complex equations. She's not a mathematical savant, but her parents initially thought she was, because she could answer increasingly complex equations. Then they learned she doesn't know the answer unless the person working with her does.

> This startling discovery was made by her therapist while doing math exercises. Without seeing the calculator, or being told of the change, Hayley's answers switched from ordinary numbers to scientific notation… right after the display on the therapist's calculator changed in the same way. When asked how she had done that, Hayley typed back, "I see the numerators and

denominators in your head."

Hayley then answered many questions she shouldn't have known the answers to, such as the surname of her therapist's landlord, and the name of a book the therapist was thinking about. Hayley was correct each time.

On her side of a wooden barrier, Hayley identifies what the therapist is seeing, on the other side, with more than 90% accuracy. This is a much higher score than in any of the successful experiments cited in Part 3.

Powell has proceeded to study and quantify the phenomenon under strict and repeatable conditions. On Vimeo, watch "The Telepathy Project" and "Compiled Telepathy Experiment Samples."

Powell also worked with an autistic boy.

> I generated a list of random words, and I had that on my computer, which was out of sight of the boy. I gave the mother the words one at a time, she thought them toward him, and he just typed each one out accurately. It's extremely powerful to see this boy just sitting there typing, and then to see the words show up on the screen. It's *chilling*.

After working with several other similarly gifted children, Powell has come to the conclusion that

> the data are highly suggestive of an alternative, latent and/or default communication mechanism that can be accessed by people born with severely impaired language abilities. The implications of telepathy are so profound that it is met with fierce opposition, even though many Nobel laureates and other eminent scientists have supported it for over a century. Most scientists don't want to go out on a limb and look into it.

A Brain Upgrade

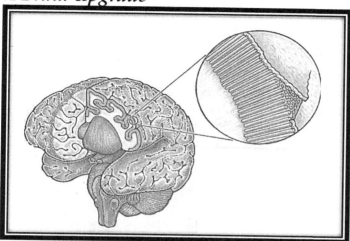

Minicolumns

In the same interview, Powell explains that

> in the autistic brain, rather than the cerebral cortex dominating the deeper structures, there's less of that top-down inhibition. Also, the frontal lobes are not as engaged as in neurotypical thinkers. There's comparatively more information processing that occurs in the posterior structures than the anterior. It seemed to me that this kind of functioning would make it more likely for a person to be able to tap into a primal capacity such as telepathy. [The posterior structures are far older in evolutionary terms.]

> For [an extraordinary claim to be taken seriously], you have to really ground it in science that's already accepted. I see that as

my mission, not only to understand what consciousness is and what these abilities are but also to specify the brain's role in it. There's a reason why we're not all experiencing these things all the time, and why some people do.

I can tell you one thing that is very different about their brain. There's something called a minicolumn, which is like a microprocessor. If you look at the minicolumns in their brain, they have more of them and they're also more compact, more dense. As a result, they have an "upgrade," so to speak.

I checked this out and, being a neuroscientist, Powell is correct. At the Autism Science Foundation's website, we read that

> Minicolumns are the basic unit of information processing in the brain. In Autism Spectrum Disorder, these minicolumns are between 5% and 10% wider than in those without autism. This difference may not sound like much, but multiplied over hundreds of thousands of minicolumns throughout the brain it may contribute to a significant difference in brain organization. This may explain the altered cognitive style or focus in many people with autism.[45]

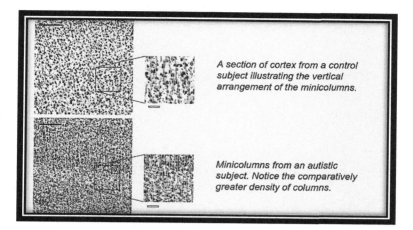

A section of cortex from a control subject illustrating the vertical arrangement of the minicolumns.

Minicolumns from an autistic subject. Notice the comparatively greater density of columns.

My prediction? When a Sasquatch brain is inevitably scanned or dissected, we will find it to be loaded with extra-dense minicolumns—inherited from our ancient common ancestor—and their hindbrain and visual cortex will be larger and more developed, in comparison to the cerebral cortex, than those of our own species.

Fields of Knowing

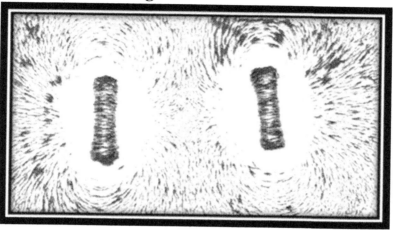

"When I think about consciousness," Powell continues, switching to the nature of telepathy generally,

> I'm thinking about all this information that's stored in a field. Think about a magnet under a piece of paper with a lot of iron filings. They will arrange themselves in a very organized array around that magnet. But we wouldn't otherwise see the force...if we didn't have those filings there on that piece of paper.
>
> I think of consciousness as being like that, this highly organized field that contains information. It's in the body and out of the body, both. It's not just contained within the body. Some people think of the brain in the most concrete way, as a bunch of chemicals. And so, if what you're wondering is how *this* bag of chemicals communicates with *that* bag

of chemicals, it doesn't work. If that's *really* how you think of the brain, as just what you buy at the grocery store in the organ section, of course it can't be telepathic — that's ridiculous! Why even discuss it? But if what it is is an informational field, then it can be in contact with other informational fields.

A lot of people are familiar with the concept of *entanglement*, which Dean Radin and others have popularized. So if you think about it, a field can be entangled with another field. In that sense, you can, within your field, tap into where it's entangled with that other field. It's not like you're sending something outside of yourself. Instead, think of it as a microcosm; your consciousness field is a microcosm of the larger field, and because of that you can tap into others within it.

Creatures in the Field

A common observation by people living at habituation sites or walking through an active Sasquatch area is the strange behavior of animals. Often, for instance, they notice that birds, especially crows, will come abnormally close, sometimes within a few feet, and just stare at them. Marc Abell (Colorado Bigfoot on YouTube) has documented this phenomenon in such videos as "Huge Raven/Crow" and "Graceland, Followed by a crow for 30 min." He believes that the Sasquatch are actually looking at him, keeping tabs on his actions, *through the eyes of* woodland creatures, using them as intermediaries — and he is not alone, as we'll see below. But how can such a thing be true?

Well, the very same way that telepathy is true for us and for Sasquatch. Indeed, if autistic savant gifts tend to correlate with psychic abilities in our own species, then nature may be repeating herself—or better: *agreeing* with herself—in the case of animals. Consider the nearly photographic memory of birds (like the Clark's nutcracker) that hide tens of thousands of seeds in the fall, up to twenty miles from their home ground, and then relocate them in midwinter; consider the crow's practical smarts in YouTube's "Are Crows the Ultimate Problem-Solvers? | Inside the Animal Mind | BBC Earth"; consider the visual intelligence of the chimpanzee, which far outstrips that of our own kind when it comes to immediate working memory, as shown in the astonishing video out of Kyoto, Japan, "Chimp vs Human! | Memory Test | BBC Earth."

These are three salient examples among many that I could cite, but the point is that most animals possess types of intelligence that we—or not the *average* (neurotypical)

human being at least—simply do not. Moreover, many of their capacities tend to converge with those of autistic savants. In *Animals in Translation: Using the Mysteries of Autism to Decode Animal Behavior,* famed autistic writer Temple Grandin, who has spent her lengthy career helping us to understand our fellow creatures, speaks of "animal genius" and even goes so far as to assert that "in a sense, animals *are* autistic savants."[46]

Not surprisingly, then, researchers have found that some also prove adept at telepathy. Most prominent among these is Rupert Sheldrake, whose experiments with dogs can be tasted in the YouTube videos "Jaytee, a dog who knew when his owner was coming home: The ORF Experiment" and "Richard Wiseman's failed attempt to debunk the 'psychic pet' phenomenon." For a much richer meal, see Sheldrake's book *Dogs That Know When Their Owners Are Coming Home.*[47]

Above, I mentioned that others, besides Marc of Colorado Bigfoot, have felt that Sasquatch work through animals to monitor and make contact with us. Not only does this make sense in the context of Powell's "information fields" — because minds produce and participate in these regardless of brain size — but it also resonates with the savant-telepathy nexus. Moreover, it appears that species categories do not limit the flow of information or divide the hive.

Elizabeth (whom we met in Part 2) relates the following three experiences
One day, this cat showed up out of the blue. She was feral. I'd go out and she'd back off. I'd throw her food and she'd come and eat it with one eye on the food and one eye on me. One night, I was sitting out on the porch in my chair, and it was dark, and here comes this cat running up, and she jumped into my lap. I'm thinking, *What is going on here?* She was looking me right in the eye. I said, "What is wrong with you?" I tried to pull her off, but she was hanging on just like Velcro. I couldn't get her loose from me.

Finally, I said, "Brocky [a local Sasquatch], do you have something to do with this?" I heard a noise past the tree line, so I knew it was her that was doing it. I sat and rubbed the cat and rubbed the cat and talked to her, and then in a little bit I quit hearing the noises in the woods, and at that time the cat's eyes got big and she jumped off of me and off of the porch and out into the yard and just went tearing off. Like she was hypnotized and then came back to herself. I think they were looking through her eyes.

I think they used my duck the same way, and he hated it. We had a wood duck as a pet for seven years. Once a year, in springtime, there'd be a gathering of the Bigfoot, and there'd be a whole lot of new ones here, and they'd all want to see inside the house, and they'd look through the duck's eyes. He'd sit there and look around, up at the ceiling, go in another room and look around. (This was not his typical behavior at all; he liked to just sit around on one leg with his head under his wing.) Then he'd come back and look at me like he'd never seen me before. It was like it wasn't even him in there. Then he got to where he'd get mad when they'd do that to him. This was before I could talk to them.

One night, I decided to make a little teepee and see if they would add to it or whatever. I found three sticks, about three feet long and leaned them together to make the teepee.

The next morning, I went out to see what had happened and was surprised to find a *rabbit* sitting inside of it. There was another rabbit sitting beside it, but it ran off when I got close. The one in the teepee just sat there like it didn't see me. I kicked some leaves at it, but it didn't move, so I poked it with a stick and it just sat there like it was hypnotized. Finally, I said "What is wrong with you? Are you crazy?" When I spoke, it shot out of there like a rocket and disappeared into the bushes.

I couldn't ask the Bigfoot about it then — this was before mindspeak — and pondered it for years, but then one of the older ones that was a kid here back then has grown up and is back now with his family. I asked him what caused the rabbit to do that and heard him laughing. He said, "We put a spell on the teepee to catch the rabbit. You didn't think we run them down, did you?"

Robin (also from Part 2) adds these accounts
During my lifetime with the Foots, I have noticed a lot of contact between them and other animals. The Foots around me have always used coyotes, fox, and even raccoons as pets and go-betweens. I know of some that even have cougars as pets. They use the animals as pets very similar to what we do. Not only to cuddle, pet, and love but also as guard pets. These animals respond to the Foots just as our pets do to us.

Another way they are used is to move forward in an area before the Foots come in. They will check to make sure the area is safe for them, often sending them in as scouts before entering themselves.

When I put food out there have been times when they would send the same three raccoons in to check and see what food was offered as well as if the coast was clear. The raccoons would enter the feeding area, go to each bucket of table scraps and what-not, and check for food. *They never once touched any of the food.* They would then go to the top of the tallest tree in the feeding area, and the largest raccoon would make a screaming noise towards the area that the Foots would come in from. Then all three would climb down the tree and leave, going in a direction away from the Foots' area so they never crossed paths with them. After the raccoons left, the Foots would come and take the food. It would be literally a matter of minutes. This has happened many, many times. It became a pattern, and I was used to it happening.

They have also at times sent a fox to my house to check on me. I would not be feeling well, and a red fox would show up outside my door as if standing guard. I would go to the door and it would look at me then back off about ten to fifteen feet from the door, lay down, and just watch the house.

One day, I was outside sitting near our burn pit. We had had our kids and grandkids over the night before and had a bonfire and roasted marshmallows and hot dogs. I went out to pick up a few things left outside. I had left marshmallows and hot dogs out for the Foots on one of the benches as well as a few left-over cans of soda. I was picking up the now-empty wrappers from the marshmallows and the empty, crunched cans of soda. I decided to sit for a min. When I did, seven field mice came out from the woods in a straight line and walked directly to my feet, looking at me. Then they went right back to the woods as if they were reporting something to someone. When I looked up, all I saw was the back of a furry head about eight feet off the ground and heard branches and brush crunching.

Another time, I was putting food into all of their food buckets and three deer came from the direction of the

Foots and walked right up to me. They looked at the situation and then walked off. They were within inches of me where I could have touched them. I simply stood there knowing they were checking things out and let them do what they needed to. Right after that I head whoop calls the Foots were making to each other.

There have been countless situations I have seen them use other animals. They have sent crows as well as hawks to spy on people, including myself. This can be from the bad Foots as well as the good. The bad ones will use animals to watch what we are doing as well. They seem to be able to control by mind anyone or anything they wish. I'm not saying they do this a hundred percent of the time. In fact, they only do it if they need to. However, they will use any animal as a pet. They also control our pets. If they need them to be quiet they will put them to sleep. Or they can call them to themselves. I have had them do that with my dogs and cats many times. They have a way of calming any animal or terrifying them. whatever suits their needs.

A Dance of Distraction

Coyote

Sasquatch

August 17, 2015, will stick with me forever. That's the day I stumbled into the middle of a drama in the ravine where I'd been researching. (See YouTube: "Sasquatch Up Close and Personal: My Two Years of Learning in the Ravine.") Little suspecting I'd someday write this book, its main theme touched down right in front of me.

As soon as I arrived that morning, the silence was broken by the howl of a coyote from somewhere just above me on the ridge. Immediately afterward came a series of clear wood knocks, though I didn't notice them at the time; one can hear them on the video "Morning Visits 2015: The Juvenile Sasquatch Footage."

I howled back, and then the coyote let loose with a long, gorgeous succession of responses, which was followed, in turn, again, by an obvious Sasquatch signal—this time a single knock.

As I sat facing the steep bank of the ravine, and much to my surprise, within a minute or so the howler actually trotted down the slope into view and stood there calmly looking at me. This was no Sasquatch but exciting nonetheless; what naturally skittish wild creature casually *approaches* a person? I filmed the visit, which lasted for fourteen seconds before the animal turned and dashed back uphill and over the ridgetop.

That's when I began to hear branches snapping from somewhere out of sight, up near where the coyote had disappeared, and then a light wood knock. *That's weird*, I thought. *Or not so weird?*

I remembered a plausible theory going around that Sasquatch and coyotes are "companion species," like humans and dogs, and that they often use teamwork to hunt together. Researchers have recorded many instances of long, low, non-canid howls followed by the yipping and shrieking of a coyote chorus. One can well imagine a pack killing a deer or other prey and having the carcass then snatched away by a gang of two-legged superiors who'd been trailing just behind or waiting on the perimeter. And really, why would the upright crew *not* make use of such easily available assistance? I'm not sure how the favor goes both ways, though, unless they share meat with their four-legged hunting partners as well—like scraps from a dinner table.

But though I heard these Sasquatch "tells" above me and scanned for the source, I failed to notice what was right under my nose, down here on my own level, just eight-eight feet away and hiding behind a small, sparse pine tree. The coyote and the invisible woodplay had successfully conspired to distract my attention so that the juvenile, who'd been caught out in a careless moment by my sudden, camera-bearing appearance, could escape the dire consequences. If my eyes were only sharper, my mind more acute, I'd have obtained footage rivaling that of Roger Patterson.

Human attention is feeble and readily swayed, and animals can evidently be brought in to exploit this weakness.

Fruits of the Gift 1

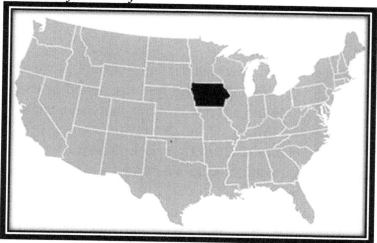

Jessie Connie's granddaughter and Tracy's niece, both featured in Part 2. She is high-functioning autistic and, according to Connie, has always been far more tuned in to the local Sasquatch group than any other member of the family.

They've done it ever since I was a little girl, six or seven. Pictures and voices both. They would put pictures in my head and talk to me. I had one that would constantly yell my name, and I'd say, "Grandma, are you yelling my name?" She wasn't. They would telepathically tell me to come outside onto the porch, and they would talk to me.

Down over the hill there used to be an old bus, and they called that their "playground." There were a bunch of sticks and children's toys in it. They'd leave markers around there to let us know that "We are the good people." Markers like little crosses, laid on the ground.

They left me magnetic rocks that stuck together. One time, they left them in a U-shape on the fence.

And I'd go out and get them toys, give them toys, and they would play with them. I gave them a couple flutes. They would take them off the wishing well, and I would find them in the cornfield.

We'd put stuffed animals on the wishing well, and they'd get moved around.

When I got older, I had a little Dodge Neon. One time, I thought my brother's girlfriend had her period in the back seat, then I found out it was one of the Sasquatches, *her* period.

They ruined all my CDs. They took them out of the thing and played with them because they were shiny and they liked the reflection.

There was this one tall black one, and his face was all greasy, and he left a big face mark on the front window of our house.

I feel like I had special access to the Bigfoot. I never felt threatened by them. They always protected me. When I would walk down to the mouth of the creek, they would follow me down there to make sure I didn't get hurt.

I had physical interactions too. I could sit and talk to them not far away. My grandma says I'm the only one out of the family that they were close to and talked to on a daily basis. When I'd be walking in the woods, they would follow me, the little ones would, and I would talk to them. I sometimes felt closer to them than to human beings.

There was one that really liked me, and his name was Kwa-eechi. Another one was Baby Boy. They said they went up to the "north country" to get Baby Boy a mate, and her name was Licorice.

I live in an apartment complex in the city now, but whenever I go back to the woods, I can re-connect with them. I can see them coming in, and I can sit near them. Not everybody has the ability to do that. I'm different. I'm autistic, high-functioning, high-learning. I'm good at memorizing things.

My grandma would ask me, "What are they trying to say?" I would tell her, and she would be surprised because they'd tell me a lot more than they would tell her. Everything I said from them turned out to be true.

They would tell me if someone in the family was sick before they even got sick, or if they were going to pass away. They would give me the heads-up. It never freaked me out when it would happen because I already knew it was true, I was aware. They told me a week before my great-grandmother passed away.

Fruits of the Gift 2

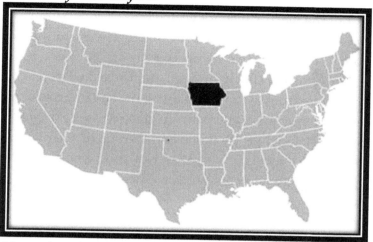

I interviewed Rick Reles on "The Nearness of You Podcast: Episode #11."

I was with an autistic man, late-twenties, named Sam. He carried a notebook and was very focused on taking notes on everything, very focused on *order*. In the group, you had to be careful not to invade his space, which was fascinating to me.

My first trip with him was also his inaugural Sasquatch outing. We were in northeastern Iowa where the glaciers have formed a lot of valleys so that you may have miles and miles of cornfields and all of a sudden you go into a canyon area.

So this night, there were ten of us. We'd gone into a canyon area that had washed out and hadn't been used much in years. We went in there *because* of that. We drove down there, and we had to go over where the water had washed out and the creeks had run over the dirt trails going in, so…very remote. We went in at night, but who goes in there? Maybe a couple kids parking once in a while, but the place is just not visited.

So we got there in the basin of this east-west-running canyon and climbed out of our vehicles…and we immediately heard knocks, immediately heard whoops.

They were from the east and the west. The impression I got was that people don't show up at ten o'clock at night. I think the Bigfoots pretty much had the run of the place themselves. As soon as we got out of the vehicles and started to talk about what we were hearing, our friend Sam started to tell us things like "There's one on the ridge above us to the north, to the north, he sees us."

And then he would start posing questions, like "They want to know why we're all here. They want to know why there's so many of us. Why are we here at night? They want to know." It wasn't like we asked him to take this role, he just started to say it. And he didn't have difficulty getting the sentences out or the inquiries. They wanted to know what the equipment we had was. We had parabolic mics and night vision. And we had red headlamps on. They wanted to know about the red lights. "Why are there red lights?" Sam said.

He was just posing questions to the group. It wasn't threatening. And we were hearing whistles, whoops, knocks. And one would come from the east side of the canyon, and then a response from the west. And we're in the middle of all this. We're down in the lower part where the water is, in this flat down there.

So I thought, *I'm going to see if he can be like a UN interpreter, so let's get the dialogue going.* I said to him, "Tell them it's okay, we don't mean any harm. Tell them we're just here because we're interested in them. They fascinate us. We're curious. Tell them we're not hunters." So he did! Some out loud, and some in his mind. He would tell them those things, and he would write down things in his book. He would step away from the group and he'd be talking.

He was getting information back. I said to him at one point, "How many are there, and where are they?" And he pointed east, and he pointed west, and he said, "They're up there, and they're down here." Right where we heard the whoops and the knocks from.

And I said, "Is it a family, is it a group?"

And he said, "It's a family. They are related, but it's also a group. It's bigger than that."

All of this was good information because it wasn't singular, even though he had pointed out that there was a sentry above us that saw us. He said at one point, "There's young and there's old." He was relaying to us things about the demographics of the situation. He pointed up and down the canyon where they were.

It went from concern at first as to why we were there and what we were doing to…it calmed down over the time we were in there. So our group started to walk up a washout road that ran north, and one of the young guys—he was there with his dad—started to get an uncomfortable feeling. He didn't want to go any further. And a couple of the others in the group said the same thing. Everybody stopped at the same time.

We had heard them in the woods like we were being paralleled. So again, I figured I'm going to use our interpreter. I said, "What's going on?"

He said, "Well, they don't want you to go up here. This is their area." And again, you could tell it was genuine because he would just repeat what he "heard." It was immediate. So we'd ask a question through him, and he'd think it or he'd ask out loud, step to the side, and he would just quickly say these things. "Up here, this is their place. Their place is up there."

I said, "Okay. Well, again, we don't mean any harm. We're just walking around. We're interested. Is it okay if we proceed further up this road? Do they want us to go back somewhere?"

"They want you to go back," Sam reported. So we turned and went back down this road, and there was a picnic area in the center of this canyon, and we sat for a while. With our parabolics, we could hear them moving above us. We saw some eye glow, eye shine, it was very obvious. You could see double-red, inquiring-type eyes. And they'd move from one area to another.

We sat there probably forty-five minutes to an hour. We would report to each other what we were hearing or seeing. You could hear through the parabolics footsteps above, moving, so we knew they were there. And clearly there were a couple of groups of them, the east and west group. They were around us, but they were jockeying for position. It wasn't threatening. It was just like there was a pause we needed to take, and we were all listening.

We heard up and down the canyon from the east and west whoops back and forth, so the two groups were talking with each other, and we had heard some knocks, a few whistles. But we hadn't heard any howls, no loud howls. I said, "Well, maybe there's no *need* for a howl if they're able to communicate with less." Someone in our group said, "Let's do a howl." I said, "No, no, no, we don't want to do that. You get more with honey than you do with vinegar."

I said to Sam, "Ask them why they haven't chosen to howl." He conveyed this and then he turned to us and said, "Just wait a minute." Literally within seconds, from the east side of the canyon, we got this seven-second-long howl.

Everybody was just dumbfounded. Then, we got up and started to move around a bit and went back to the road that was going north. Our friend Sam said, "It's okay, you can walk now." It was like they'd calmed down and were accepting of us. The whole mood of everything calmed down, and we didn't get that heavy feeling anymore. So we walked the trail and broke into two groups. I took the lead group a good hundred yards ahead of the group behind, and we were on walkie-talkie with each other. Just walking along, staying in touch. The group behind all of a sudden calls us and says, "We're stopped because large rocks are coming out of the woods and landing on the trail in front of us."

So then, our interpreter Sam just blurts this out. "Oh, there's two juveniles in the woods there. They're just having fun. They're laughing. They won't hit you with any rocks. They're just throwing them to see if they can scare us. They're laughing, just having fun."

I think they realized we didn't mean any harm. I always go back to what the Native Americans say: "Treat them with respect. Let them know you respect them." And it seems to work, and in this case, they accommodated.

The next day, we went back into the area, and one of our more adventurous members climbed up into the woods, and just where Sam had said there was a sentry, he found a rock outcropping above us, exactly where he said. And he found footprints and parts of a dead deer — the sentry had something to eat while he was sitting there watching.

Big Bang, Back Yard

© 2014 DAVID A. CLAERR

Quantum physicist David Bohm, whom we touched on earlier, speaks of two levels or "orders" of reality: explicate (explicit) and implicate (implicit). Ordinarily, we only perceive the explicit order, what's immediately before our senses, the contents and texture of everyday reality; these Bohm sees as "surface phenomena...mere approximations of an underlying process."[48]

This strikes me as analogous to how Sasquatch, covert in our world, are perpetually on the verge of showing through from "the other side of the tapestry" before returning once again to veiled potential.

Mindspeak, however, is not just *analogous* to Bohm's implicate order, to quantum reality — it is literally *made possible by it*. Even our most private conversations are continuous with the universe around us because "All particles in the history of the cosmos have interacted." In *The Nonlocal Universe*, historian of science Robert Nadeau and physicist Menas Kafatos proclaim that

Everything in our immediate physical
environment is made up of quanta that
have been entangling with other quanta
from the Big Bang to the present. This
suggests that all of physical reality is a
single quantum system.[49]

This "system," of course, includes your own back
yard, your "immediate physical environment," and the
inner sanctum of your mind. It is trying to reach you. It
is both intimate and remote. Listen in. Listen now.

References

1. Noël, Christopher, *Next of Kin Next Door: How to Find Sasquatch a Stone's Throw Away*. CreateSpace, 2018. pp. 64-66.
2. Eleftheriades, G., and Selvanayagam, M. "Experimental Demonstration of Active Electromagnetic Cloaking." *Physical Review X*, November 12, 2013.
3. Radin, Dean, *Entangled Minds: Extrasensory Experience in a Quantum Reality*. Simon & Schuster, 2006, p. 120.
4. *Ibid.*, p. 127.
5. Turing, Alan, *Computing Machinery and Intelligence. Mind, A Quarterly Review of Psychology and Philosophy*. Volume LIX, Issue No. 236, entire issue, 1950.
6. Schmidt, S., Schneider, R., Utts, J., and Walach, H. "Distant Intentionality and the Feeling of Being Stared at: Two Meta-analyses." *British Journal of Psychology*, 95, pp. 235-247.
7. Kittenis, M., Caryl, P., and Stevens, P., "Distant Psychophysiological Interaction Effects between Related and Unrelated Participants." *Proceedings of the Parapsychological Association Convention*, 2004, pp. 67-76.
8. Standish, L.J., Kozak, L., Johnson, C., and Richards, T., "Electroencephalographic Evidence of Correlated Event-Related Signals Between the Brains of Spatially And Sensory Isolated Human Subjects." *The Journal of Alternative and Complementary Medicine*, Volume 10, Number 2, 2004, pp. 307–314.
9. Jacobsen, Annie, *Phenomena: The Secret History of the U.S. Government's Investigations into Extrasensory Perception and Psychokinesis*. Little, Brown, 2017, p. 177.
10. *Ibid.*, p. 179.

11. From Einstein's preface to the German edition of *Mental Radio*, 1930.
12. "Third Eye Spies with Russell Targ." YouTube, New Thinking Allowed with Jeffrey Mishlove, published November 12, 2018.
13. Jacobsen, *Op. sit.*, pp. 234-235.
14. See Wikipedia at "Panpsychism."
15. Watson, Lyall, *Lifetide: A Biology of the Unconscious.* Hodder and Stoughton, 1979.
16. Woollaston, Victoria, "Are we all Psychic? Scientists Believe that Animals — Including Humans — Have a Collective Consciousness." The Daily Mail, sott.net, November 19, 2013
17. Global Consciousness Project, noosphere.princeton.edu.
18. Radin, *Op. sit.*, pp. 195-206
19. Talbot, Michael, *The Holographic Universe.* Harper Collins, 1991, p 34.
20. Ball, Philip, "The Strange Link Between the Human Mind and Quantum Physics." BBC.com, February 16, 2017.
21. Jahn, R.G., Dunne, B.J., Nelson, R.D., Dobyns, Y.H., and Bradish, G.J. "Correlations of Random Binary Sequences with Pre-Stated Operator Intention: A Review of a 12-Year Program." *Journal of Scientific Exploration,* 11 (3), 1997, pp. 345-367.
22. Radin, *Op. sit.*, pp.156-157.
23. Radin, *Op. sit.*, pp. 221-222.
24. Wackerman, J., "Dyadic Correlations between Brain Functional States: Present Facts and Future Perspectives." *Mind and Matter,* 2, (1), 2004, pp. 105-122.
25. Talbot, *Op. sit.*, p. 38.
26. Bohm, David, *The Undivided Universe: An Ontological Interpretation of Quantum Theory.* With B.J. Hiley, Routledge, 1993.
27. Radin, *Op. sit.*, pp. 231-32
28. Radin, *Op. sit.*, p. 235.

29. Barnard, William G., *Living Consciousness: The Metaphysical Vision of Henri Bergson.* SUNY Press, 2012, p. 253.
30. Radin, *Op. sit.*, p. 258.
31. Buchanan, Joseph Rodes, *Manual of Psychometry — The Dawn of a New Civilization.* FH Hodges,1893, p. 73.
32. MacIsaac, Tara, "Do Inanimate Objects Have Thoughts and Feelings?" *The Epoch Times,* epochtimes.com, 2014.
33. Williams, Donna, *Exposure Anxiety: The Invisible Cage: An Exploration of Self-Protection in the Autism Spectrum and Beyond.* Jessica Kingsley Publishers, 2003, p. 252
34. *Ibid.*, p.183.
35. *Ibid.*, p. 40.
36. *Ibid.*, p. 71.
37. *Ibid.*, p. 178.
38. *Ibid.*, p. 71.
39. Sandin, S., Lichtenstein, P., Kuja-Halkola, R., et alia, "The Heritability of Autism Spectrum Disorder." *Journal of the American Medical Association,* posted at JamaNetwork.com, September 26, 2017.
40. Harris, John, RewiringNeuroscience.com.
41. Reser, Jaren Edward, "Conceptualizing the Autism Spectrum in Terms of Natural Selection and Behavioral Ecology: The Solitary Forager Hypothesis." *Evolutionary Psychology,* vol. 21, issue 9(2), 2011, pp. 207-38.
42. Powell, Diane Hennacy, *The ESP Enigma: The Scientific Case for Psychic Phenomena.* Walker Publishing Company, 2009, p. 145.
43. Powell interviewed by Jannecke Oinaes on her show, "Wisdom from North," YouTube, published September 7, 2016.

44. Rimland, B., and Fein, D., "Special Talents of Autistic Savants," in *The Exceptional Brain*, Guildord Press, 1988, pp. 474-492.
45. Autism Science Foundation, "Minicolumns, Autism, and Age: What it Means for People with Autism." autismsciencefoundation.wordpress.com, August 30, 2015.
46. Grandin, Temple, *Animals in Translation: Using the Mysteries of Autism to Decode Animal Behavior*, Harcourt, 2006, p. 288.
47. Sheldrake, Rupert, *Dogs That Know When Their Owners Are Coming Home*, Broadway Books, 2011.
48. Wikipedia at "Implicate and Explicate Order."
49. Nadeau, R., and Kafatos, M., *The Nonlocal Universe: The New Physics and Matters of the Mind*. Oxford University Press, 2001, p. 81.

Christopher Noël holds a master's degree in philosophy from Yale and has dedicated the past thirteen years to learning about the Sasquatch species. He is the author of several books on the subject, including, most recently, *The Sasquatch Savant Theory; Next of Kin Next Door: How to Find Sasquatch a Stone's Throw Away; The Mind of Sasquatch and the Secret to Their Success;* and *A Field Guide to Sasquatch Structures: The 50 Most Common Types in North American Forests.* Noël lives in Vermont's Northeast Kingdom with his daughter and can be reached at MindspeakBook@gmail.com.

Made in the USA
Middletown, DE
07 October 2021